EVICTION NOTICE

10 Steps to Putting Guilt and Shame Out of Your Life

Erica N. Williams

For information regarding:
Copyright
Bulk purchases discount
Event booking
Contact evictwitherica@gmail.com

To: Malik

For all the nights you understood Mom was on a mission. For the nights you had to do homework on your own, have a simple sandwich for dinner and tuck yourself in but not before giving me what you called a "hard work" hug. I couldn't have done this without your support and encouragement. I love you more and more each day.

TABLE OF CONTENTS

ACKNOWLEDGEMENTS

I usually skip acknowledgements too. I know this is the part where the author thanks everyone who helped write the book but didn't actually write the book. I don't know those people so if you didn't bother reading this section, I wouldn't blame you.

I choose to acknowledge you, the reader. For some reason you picked up this book and for that, you are the real MVP.

I am also excited for you! You are either about to move on from something heavy or trying to keep from getting heavy and for that, I am proud of you. I'm going to share with you a few tricks to get guilt and shame out of your life. AND I'll give you a glimpse into what my life looked like before my very own eviction.

On some days I wondered if it would be easier to keep living life as I had been. I gonna be honest with you because that's what you'll have to do with yourself in reading Eviction Notice. Be desperately honest (not just regular honest) with yourself so that you are able to examine the hard areas of your life and trust God to make them better.

Next, God. I definitely have to acknowledge Him. This idea came from Him. Throughout this book I hope to give utmost reverence to God because He directed the psycho thriller that was my pre-eviction life and gave me the w

I don't have a degree of theology, psychology or any other "gy" I have no letters behind my name. As a matter of fact, I'm a college dropout. I'm not someone trying to tell you what to do or how to live from the outside looking in. I'm a person who God has personally delivered and like our grandmothers have always said "If God can do it for me, He can do it for you."

I do respect other religions and am glad that we live in a time where most people can worship whoever they feel freely. I don't think that if you read his book and you aren't a Christian then you won't be able to get anything from it. I think that the tools I developed can be useful to everyone. They are pretty simple. However, I don't know how well you will hold up without the power of God behind you.

Now to that list of names of people you guys don't know personally or how much they have helped me in writing this book. I want to acknowledge my family who accepted me with loving arms after I had turned my back on them, Pastor Kendall and First Lady Wyvetta Granger of New Life Community Church (East St. Louis, IL), my wonderful church members, my friends Mary and Genia for reading draft after draft, Vern for editing my first draft, Portlyn for keeping me encouraged and focused, Andrea and Andre for telling me to give up my social life until I completed the book and last but not least, Kim West for guiding me through an eviction neither us really knew was happening.

PRE- EVICTION PRAYER

I hope you weren't enticed by this book because you are a super-saved, holier-than-thou, better-than-them-other-folks Christian because I didn't write this book for you. I wrote this book for the down and out, can't see a way out, all messed up, broken down, cast aside folks. I want each and every one of you to know that I have prayed many prayers for you. I was depressed. I thought about suicide every day.

If you think that reading this book will be a one stop shop for fixing your life, you have the wrong book. It will shine a light down a dark hallway. You have to be willing to take the steps. Even with a flashlight in hand, walking down a dark hallway is scary. That's why we're going to invite God to take this walk with us.

Father God,

Thank you you for this time. Thank you for taking the wheel. Thank you for this road map. You know the situations at had but I know that noting is too hard for you. Give strength, encouragement, peace and deliverance. See us through. I ask you to give them faith to believe in Your Word, to see that they are special, one of a kind and created with a purpose. Give them your eyes to see themselves more clearly to see who you intended them to be.

In the name of Jesus I pray,

Amen

ONE

INTRODUCTION

April, 2012

The sermon in church was just about how God can bring you back from death or whatever for that matter and it spoke to me. I have to let go and let God. I have to get rid of this guilt and just let it go. I don't want my attitude to become nonchalant about life because that's not how I feel. I just want to be able to embrace life for what it is. Maybe I need therapy, I mean I don't think I'm a sociopath or anything but I do need someone to discuss things with and then dismiss them, moving on with my life.

When we feel ashamed about something it takes over our thoughts and if we aren't careful, our lives. Many people fall into a sort of functioning depression or moral traps because of something they have done and don't' want people to know about. These things lead to low self-esteem, the desire and need to please people fir approval, even suicide.

For these reasons, we are about to embark on a journey of eviction. Together we are going to get guilt and shame out of your head and your life. God has provided me with the vision of comparing what He did in my life to an eviction. I'm sure we all know what the eviction process is.

Someone moves into a house or apartment with plans to stay for an agreed on length of time, for an agreed on amount of rent or payment. They stop paying rent or do something outside of the terms and conditions and the property owner files a lawsuit, presents the evidence to the court and if they win the case the tenant moves out peacefully OR the landlord gets help from local law enforcement with removing the tenant from the property.

On this journey our minds and our hearts are the property. Guilt and shame are the tenants. We are going to evict them. Simple it seems, but God wants this to be crystal clear. So let's start with defining a few things.

Eviction: the process of expelling, especially a tenant, from a property; expulsion.

Expel: to deprive someone (or something) involvement in a school or organization.

Deprive: to deny the possession or use of something.

Possession: the state of owning or controlling something, being controlled by a demon or spirit.

Let's make 2+2+2+2=8. Because we are giving guilt and shame an EVICTION, we are going to EXPEL them from our property, our minds. This means, we are going to DEPRIVE them of the right to be involved in our lives. We are going to deny them the right to POSSESS us, therefore denying them the right to control us.

With an eviction process, we will have to prove what damage has been done. We will explore guilt, shame, sub-Tenants and assess the damages they have caused. At the end of each chapter we will collect data in a section called "Grounds for Eviction". During these sections you will be presented with simplistic, thought provoking questions that will cause you to think and inspire action. You can answer the questions outright or use another creative outlet such as poetry, music or art.

Additionally, there will be opportunities for you to take a break or "recess" from the eviction process and recollect yourself. Your recess will consist of journaling pages that you can use to express yourself. I have provided prompts to get your juices going and help you think about your situations in a new way.

Drudging up past events or going into deep thought about current events can be heavy. To encourage you will be affirmations or sayings that you can use to get you through each phase of the eviction. At the end of each chapter take a moment to read Re-Enforcements: Affirmations for Your Case.

Throughout the book I will share "exhibits" or real life situations from my case which will show how guilt and shame terrorized me. I will share with you some, just some, of the things I fought before I decided I had enough.

There will be multiple sections called "Preparing for Court". Obviously you won't be going to the courthouse in your town. Court will be referring to the time you spend in prayer with God that will result in the eviction. Prayer is a tool, a muscle that must be exercised and these sections are to get you stronger for that day. There will be prayer suggestions to get you ready for your court date and will relate to the content of the chapter. They can be used immediately or during your quiet time with God. I hope you are prepared.

Let's get started!

TWO

WHITEBOX CONDITION

Imagine yourself as the house of your dreams. Big and extravagant 10 bedroom, 12 bathroom mansion with parts you haven't seen since your initial tour. Big columns decorate the entrance with a stairwell and open floorplan, something that you would imagine the entrance of your very own castle would look like.

There's a lower level to the house that is larger than an entire home in the nicest suburb in town, therefore far too nice to be called a basement. When you walk in, thanks to the cleaning staff, it always smells like fresh linen and flowers, so potent that when your guests leave they smell as if they have just visited a rose garden.

Maybe your dream house, like mine, is not a house at all. It's a penthouse apartment in the middle of a great city. At night the view is enough to halt conversation, so much that the blinds are on a timer to open up at dusk. There's valet, doormen, bellhops, housekeepers, laundry service, room service and of course a life guard for the Olympic sized pool.

Using that same imagination, imagine if the inside of your mind is a house. Picture a house being inside of your skull instead of your brain. It's kind of weird isn't it? What would it be like on the inside?

In the living room would be all the things you need for day to day living, there would probably be a room for all of your childhood memories, a room for all the skills you need at school or work and maybe a room for all of your leisure time and activities. Is everything neat and tidy or is it a mess?

The condition of your house, inside and out, would be determined by who lives there. I hope you didn't think it was an empty house! You know those thoughts you have that run back and forth through your mind all day? That's who lives in your house, those are your tenants, your thoughts.

Think about all of the kinds of thoughts you have. Happy, sad, angry, mad, scary, jealous, prideful, peaceful and many, many more. If Happy is a person, how does he take care of your house? Does he sing cheerful songs and make sure others are in as good of mood that he is? Does he cook breakfast on Saturday mornings and offer to help others with their chores? What about Sad? Does she dampen the mood no matter the room she's in?

When I imagine a house where Anger lives. I can see the screen door hanging on by a thread from being slammed shut so often. I can see tire marks in the street in front of the house from Anger driving off so fast during flare ups. I imagine holes in the walls and an empty fridge because who thinks about eating during a fit of rage?

When I imagine a house where Fear lives I see a very dark place. There's no porch light or anything else to attract attention. I see heavy dark curtains and everything inside is eerily in place. It looks like no one lives there at all.

When guilt and shame lived in my house they were the worst roommates. They are kind of people that always point out when you've done something wrong. The type of people that make you feel like you might as well not even try because your efforts will be in vain. They are the kind of people that didn't comfort Sad, instead they validated her reasons. When Happy made his seldom visits they tried to bring him down. They reminded him of the one time he made breakfast and burned the eggs to convince him from not doing his Saturday morning routine.

The thoughts running around your head are all living together. Like The Real World or The Bad Girls Club, they are tenants picked to live in a house together whether they like it or not. As in most situations, when there is a group of people delegated to accomplish a task (in this case, run your life) someone has to be in charge. Who is the H.T.I.C (Head Tenant in Charge) in your house? If you are reading this book, it's probably Guilt or Shame.

Nobody wants to admit it, but the fact remains almost all of us live with or have lived with Guilt and Shame. I can go further to say that we all would rather rent to tenants like Happiness, Joy, Peace and Patience. I can imagine they all pay rent on time! So why not just invite Joy and Peace to move in? Why do we have to do an eviction?

It's important that we do an eviction because Happiness, Joy, Peace and Patience, will NOT room with Guilt and Shame. At least, not successfully.

There will continually be grief and strife because that's what Guilt and Shame attract. We have to get Guilt and Shame out of the property and clean it up before renting out the space to new tenants.

Who else gets that sinking feeling when they realize they forgot to put on deodorant? It's terrifying because if you are in a situation where you can't run to the store or don't have a random stick of deodorant in your locker or bag, you're pretty much doomed. Your mind races wondering what you can do to prevent the green fumes of stank from coming out from under your arms. You know that once that happens, your day is pretty much over. We all know that once that funk comes, you have to bathe/shower, period. There's no covering up the funk with deodorant or perfume at that point because it will only make things worse.

When we live with Guilt and Shame and invite Happiness and Joy over, that's the same result. It might work for a minute, but eventually things go from bad to worse. Guilt and Shame don't live in their rooms making cameos from time to time. They are like that mucus thing from the TV commercials that follow us around, stinking up the place and forcing us into their uncomfortable, dark spaces.

There is no way to reason with them. It is really, their way or well, their way. There is no option to leave, they are in YOUR house. Whenever guilt and shame come on the scene, they are in charge. The only way to advance comfortably is to put them out and strip down to the basics, to get to White box Condition.

In going forward with the eviction it's important to realize that transforming homes to white box condition is the ultimate goal.

When buying a house the term "white box condition" is often used to describe a home that's ready to move in. It means that the dwelling is up to code and has passed all inspections. The walls are white and ready to make your own. The options are limitless and the limits are few. You are free to transform this place into whatever it is that you would like to see to it become. You can add walls or tear them down but the main frame stays the same.

Whatever your dream house is, big mansion, city apartment or country cottage I want you to fully visualize that this dwelling represents you. Brand spanking new, complete, not lacking or wanting for anything, you are a sight to behold. There is none other like you, you are a dwelling place that is one of a kind. If an architect tried to build another house like yours, he would live his whole life in vain. This is what God saw in you when He created you and what He still sees in you today.

"Erica, this whole eviction thing is alright. I get it, but what does "white box condition" look like?"

I'm glad you asked.

"For you created my inmost being, you knit me together in my mother's womb. I praise you because I am fearfully and wonderfully made; your works are wonderful, I know that full well. My frame was not hidden from you when I was made in the secret place, when I was woven together in the depths of the earth. Your eyes saw my unformed body; all the days ordained for me were written in your book before one of them came to be." Psalms 139:13-16 (NIV)

God is the ultimate architect. He made all things, everything, breathing and non-breathing. When God made you, He was involved from the very beginning. By the time you were a kick in the stomach, a blurb on a computer screen, a heartbeat or even a fingerprint, God was already knee deep in who you would be. You were made as something to be in awe of.

I like how this version goes on to say "My frame was not hidden from you." According to Wikipedia, "In construction, framing is the fitting together of pieces to give a structure support and shape." When we apply that to us as our dream homes, our frame is the pieces of us, the pieces given by God that make up who we are. How wonderful is it that all the little things about us are not hidden from God, but PROVIDED by Him? Whether you are loud and extroverted or quiet and reserved, your entire personality and character, the very essence of who you are were provided by God.

In the respect of our homes being our mind, character will represent the condition of our home. Our character is who and what we are when no one is looking, when we first wake up in the morning, what we all boil down to. Tenants are our thoughts and our character. Therefore the condition of the home is the result of our thoughts or how our tenants behave. If you have ever said "I can't help it, it's just who I am." I want the last time you said that about yourself to be the last time.

We can change our character, we can change who we are and it starts with changing our mind, simply put, our tenants. When God made us, He also gave us the power of deciding what tenants we let in our homes.

There are certain tenants who He gave a personal invite, who He sends through the Holy Spirit. These are the tenants who will make sure our house is a home, comfortable and pleasant to all.

I'm sure we all know somebody who has worn out their welcome. If you don't, then you're probably the welcome wear-outer. The person who you plan to stay for a day or two, in their own space to not even be noticed. Three weeks later they are still there, eating the last of your favorite chips while walking around in your robe and talking to your mom about how you can do so much better in life. They are sleeping in your bed when the plan was for them to stay on the couch, not washing dishes leaving hardened ketchup on everything and (the worst offense) leaving the bathroom floor wet once they take a bath or shower.

When we do things out of guilt and shame, we may think that it's a one-time offense but they really have taken residency in your house and you didn't even know. Like the freeloading guest, they eventually go from part time guest to full time tenant and it normally happens before you even know it. When God made you, He didn't want Anger beating you down from the inside out or Guilt stinking up the place. He wanted specific tenants to live there.

"But the fruit that comes from having the Holy Spirit in our lives is: love, joy, peace, not giving up, being kind, being good, having faith, being gentle, and being the boss over our own desires. The Law is not against these things." Galatians 5:22-23 (NLV)

In other words the tenants God designed to live with you are Love, Joy, Peace, Patience, Kindness, Goodness, Faithfulness, Gentleness and Self Control. These are the tenants that will take care of your property. These are the tenants that will pay rent on time. These are the tenants that will make sure your house grows to be worth more and more each year. I can attest that if you try to invite these tenants to share a space with Guilt, Shame and Fear it will only result in chaos. When you have cleaned your property, then and only then can you invite the tenants designed to live in your space.

When Love lives with you, there is no room for Fear.

When Peace lives with you there is no room for Guilt.

When Faithfulness lives with you, there is no room for   Shame.

When Self Control lives with you, there is no room for   Anger.

The first step in living with the tenants God designed especially for you is evicting their counterparts. This is a hard thing to do because these counterparts don't want to be homeless! They will try to talk you out of evicting them that's why the first step in the eviction process is to know who you are in Christ. Knowing how special, loved and important you are to God will give you the strength and foundation you'll need to carry out this process.

"Before I shaped you in the womb, I knew all about you. Before you saw the light of day, I had holy plans for you." Jeremiah 1:5 (MSG)

God's word tells us clearly that He has a plan for us. He was talking to Jeremiah in this instance but His promises are not good for one use only. Examples of His good works are given not only that we may be in awe of Him but to strengthen our faith and know what He is capable of doing in our very own lives. This is for all of us. That includes you! The only thing that can keep us from seeing our mainframe, our purpose, is clutter and the tenants we move in our homes.

If God has a plan for us, then clearly we mean something to him. We matter. He cares about us more than we care for ourselves. He cares for us more than our own parents. I have a friend who told me that during a time of doubt God told He cares for her more than the man she married! That is because He does!

In human ways, we don't make plans for something we don't have any care about. We make plans for things that we are going to use. We plan what we are wearing and in turn take care of our clothes. We plan what we will eat and take care of our bodies. We plan to put oil and gas in our cars and take care of them. We don't make plans for useless stuff in our top kitchen drawer and we don't use it.

God wants to use us so badly. He is such a good God that He has made plans for us and already equipped us to accomplish the goal. God's word tell us many things about His plans for the Earth, His many promises to us and the compassion He has for us through the experiences of Jesus Christ. God's word also tells exactly who we are in accordance to His plan.

It says that ALL things work together for the GOOD of those who love God, it says we are called according to His purpose. No matter what happens, it will work out for the good of us because God has called us to fulfill His purpose. God has a purpose for us, His words will not come back void, they will do what they are intended to do and for that reason, no matter WHAT happens, it WILL be for the good of us. THEN we get a bonus in that on top of having a purpose and protection from God, he has also called for us to be similar to the image and likeness of Jesus, so much so that He is like our big brother!

No matter what you may be going through, no matter who has written you off, know that change is possible with God. You are already on your way. The simple truth is that we have to believe and know that God is in control and remain open to that. We have to know that our time spent on Earth is to be a reflection of Him. I believe that the first step in getting anywhere is setting a goal and to reiterate, our goal here is to get our homes in white box condition so that we can invite the tenants approved by God. Before we go further, let's examine who is living with us and who needs to go.

LET'S PRAY

Heavenly Father,

Thank you for giving me a purpose. The things that have been bad in my life can be used for good use with your power. I know that in you I am forgiven, I am purposeful and I am loved. Thank you for these gifts. Amen

GROUNDS FOR EVICTION

Knowing that God created you for a purpose, what guilt and/or shame kept you from believing that?

_____

_____

_____

_____

_____

How do you think your life will change with Guilt and Shame no longer living on your property?

_____

_____

_____

_____

_____

RE-ENFORCEMENTS: AFFIRMATIONS

I am loved.

There's always purpose in pain.

Great things are waiting for me.

RECESS: WHITEBOX CONDITION

Take a moment to really think about what white box condition really means to you. Answer 2 or more of the following questions: When was the last time you were in white box condition? What tenants moved in to change that? What do you think it will be like to be in white box condition once again? What potential barriers do you see to getting back to white box condition? What could help you overcome them?

_____
_____
_____
_____
_____
_____
_____
_____
_____
_____
_____
_____
_____

THREE

GUILT

Situations may occur and you aren't sure how to handle them based on previous experiences or what you believe other people may think. For example, your friend asks you to borrow $100. She hasn't paid you back previous loans but when you think about the fact that in college she didn't tell anyone you cheated on a test, you concede and give her the loan knowing that she won't pay you back.

Guilt by definition is "the feeling of responsibility for having done something wrong". Feeling responsible for a wrong doing is not necessarily a bad thing. In fact, in Christianity it's called conviction or revelation. That is when, through the Holy Spirit, God lets you know that you are doing or have done something wrong.

In the world we may recognize it as our conscience. It's that pain in your stomach or even your heart when you yell at your child when they don't deserve it, when you don't let a pedestrian cross in front of your car because you are in a hurry, when you take the last donut knowing you've had 3 and Carole complains about not having any. These are all good things to feel because we can learn from them if we take the right steps.

When we are operating out of guilt, we feel that there is some price to pay or punishment to serve. The thing is, under this regime nothing is ever enough.

You can never loan enough money, take enough insults or give enough compliments. Guilt continually asks for more and more of you until you are dry inside.

We are not perfect creatures and we will make mistakes or simply do the wrong thing at the wrong time. Once we understand that Jesus died on the cross specifically for those times and that our failures are no surprise to God, we can serve Guilt with the eviction notice it deserves.

Jesus paid the ultimate price, His life, so that we may live fully and abundantly. When we make mistakes and feel that pang in our stomachs, we are to go to God in prayer IMMEDIATELY. Confess your sin to God, thank Him for the revelation, ask Him to strengthen you in that area and make a wholehearted effort to give up whatever deed you committed. If need be, ask Him to send help via a mentor, book or scripture. I guarantee that is a more fulfilling life.

As a young girl, I met a lot of boys and went on a lot of dates. Most led to sex, some did not. The ones that led to sex were most often with a guy who I didn't really like but because we had been on a date or two, I felt like I had to. In these days and times there are a lot of sexually free women. Though I've always felt convicted after fornication, the desire to keep the attention of a man would often overshadow that. The next day or sometimes immediately after, I would feel so very bad. I felt like Jesus Himself would be in the room shaking His head at me. I would make a promise to not do it again but often found myself in the same situation.

That's when I would hear guilt say things like "It's not like you're a virgin anyway. He's spent his money on you, he could've been with someone else." If I tried to resist, it didn't take much convincing from the guy because guilt had won half the battle for him.

"Cling to your faith in Christ and keep your conscience clear." 1 Timothy 1:19 (NLT)

The first step in getting guilt out of your life is to go to God immediately in prayer. When you are feeling responsible for doing something wrong go to a quiet place and speak to God about it. Don't wait until you get home or until the kids go to sleep because that gives guilt time to bother you until you accept it. Go to the restroom, to your car or a quick walk down the hall and confess whatever sin you believe you are guilty of. If you are unsure if it was a sin or not and just feel bad, ask God to show you. Then ask God to help you in that area.

Once you have confessed the sin and petitioned God for help, it's best to continue living life until God sends the help you may need or strengthens you in that area. It sounds so simple but what about when that little voice comes to you and nags you, won't let you forget, won't let you live? When you confess sin, it's most often done in faith or believing in something even though you can't see it and it hasn't been done yet.

When you act on or think in accordance with that negative voice, you have committed treason, which is a breach of faith. You are no longer believing in God but believing in that voice. Here's how to counteract the Voice of Treason with the Voice of Reason.

If that voice can talk you, then you can speak back. Its science right? For every action there's an equal and opposite reaction. So if this voice speaks negativity to you, then out loud or quietly, you can speak positivity.

Guilt operates in a shady business. Nothing is ever done outright and upfront. Guilt speaks to you and the other tenants in your mind in hush tones, full of implications, suggestions and what ifs. So it's best to speak back to guilt in an outright tone. You may seem foolish when you do this out loud but when Guilt speaks to you it's important to confront those thoughts immediately. Writing out those thoughts may also help.

Plain and simple, in the Word of God, that He doesn't want you harping over things that you have and haven't done. God needs us to operate in a manner where are minds are open to hear Him and the Holy Spirit with direction for our lives. Only you can discern how the voice sounds to you but if you are steadily thinking about past mistakes you remove the opportunity to live in the fullness of God. God is almighty, He is powerful and nothing, not even you will stop His plan from meeting completion but what a joy it is to live peacefully in the meantime.

You, your life, your mind are being represented as a whole house. Guilt is only one of the tenants, taking up one room. It shouldn't be so bad, you may think.

Have you ever noticed that when someone makes another person feel guilty it's called a "guilt trip"? Why not a "guilt stop"? The answer is because Guilt isn't a one stop destination. Guilt takes you a journey to some deep, dark places that could be avoided if you just say no.

Guilt living in your house is like putting a drop of food coloring into a glass of water. You would think that so much water would overpower the food coloring, but the food coloring is so dense, so powerful, even in a droplet.

Guilt doesn't stay in its room and live peacefully. Misery loves company. Guilt goes into the rooms of Happiness, Joy, and Peace and convinces them that they are wrong and gives them things to worry about. They retreat into their rooms and Guilt takes reign, like the ring leader of your emotions. Even in a small amount, guilt is a dangerous thing. That's why we have to keep our conscience clear.

Keeping a clear conscience is not an easy thing to do. It involves looking at every situation honestly, admitting your mistakes and sometimes a weakness. If we are being honest, admitting fault or weakness is never fun and never a good feeling, but when we take those feelings to God in prayer, He can make the best of it and you can begin (or continue) to live your best life.

When we are not feeling guilty about our shortcomings, we can admit them to God and give Him what He needs to make a change in our lives. God isn't a God of force. God gives us free will to what we choose, how we choose to do it. He gives us that power because He doesn't want to control us, He wants a loving relationship with us. He wants us to love and need Him as much as He loves and needs us. Therefore, He doesn't go around just fixing this and manipulating that but allows us to petition Him for help.

My son became independent at a very early age. I'm talking two, maybe even 18 months. When I would dress him, he would try to take over and even swat my hands away because he wanted to do it himself. I wanted to help him because after all I did have a job to make it to, but letting him figure things out on his own has made him who he is today. Sitting back and watching him took tremendous restraint and still does today. However, when he asks for help then I am available, I can do something. As long as he stood there trying his hardest, not admitting that he needed any help, there was nothing I could do but watch. As long as he was trying this and trying that it seemed as though he was satisfied turning the wheels in his head to get things figured out, if he was suffering, how would I have known?

When we are having a hard time with something we can either suffer in silence or get support from the Son. Our heavenly father tells us the same thing. In 2 Corinthians 12:9 (NLT) Paul says "Each time he said "My grace is all you need. My power works best in weakness." Admitting an area of weakness, to God, is the key to eradicating guilt. What areas are you weak in? Do you take responsibility for other people's mistakes? Do you take no responsibility for your own mistakes? Are there people you can't say no to?

There are often times when a friend or family member makes us feel like if we don't help them, then who will. Maybe we have the money, the car, the alcohol, the couch to sleep on or whatever it is they need.

There is nothing wrong with helping our brothers and sister in Christ, in fact it's one of duties as Christians. You know when you are helping someone who needs it, who was sent to you by God, because there is most often a feeling of completeness that goes along with doing a good deed. When you feel taken advantage of, helpless, forced or even putting yourself in a bad situation to help them, that is when you are doing something out of guilt and no good comes from that.

In the example of a drug addict, if they continually ask you for money and you continually provide, knowing that it's not helping them, chances are you are doing it out of guilt. What if they have to commit a crime to get the drug money? Then it will be your fault for not providing it. What if you don't let her sleep at your house and she faces sleeping under a bridge? It will be your fault because you could've opened your doors for her.

When we operate in this way, it's almost like telling God he can't protect, deliver and guard this person. WE take on the role of protector and our slowly diminishing ourselves. We think about that money we gave and wonder how high is she? Is she being assaulted in a drug house because I gave her money? Do you see how whether or not the money is provided guilt finds a way to take over your thought? To distract you from you God given mission? BUT when we turn those situations over to God we have a peace that surpasses all understanding. We go on living our best lives knowing that God is with that person and trusting His plan.

Maybe a loved one died in your care or had a terrible accident. Outside of malicious murder or neglect, do you think that whether or not you forgot to change a diaper or skipped a dose of medicine played a bigger role than God Himself, the beginning and end of life?

My grandmother lived 82 years and bore 8 children. As she neared the end of her days she began to suffer and bounce back from stroke after stroke. The last one was the most damaging leaving her in a primarily vegetated state. She couldn't talk, walk or even eat relying on a G-tube for food. It was very stressful for my family, who couldn't afford nor wanted to put her in a nursing home, to arrange a care schedule with everyone pitching in where they could. As she lay on her death bed and I saw her take her last breath I wondered if there was something I could have done.

If I could have taken more shifts looking after her giving my aunt a fresher mind would we have caught something? If I would have played a more active role in interacting with her doctor would she still be here? I was a secretary in the clinic where she received her primary care after all. Could I have been on his back about keeping a closer eye on her?

As I sat on the floor at the feet of her bed which held her lifeless body, God told me that harping over what has already been done will be of no use. Did I really think so much of myself that I believed I could change what He ordered? God didn't need me to beat myself up, He needed me to call the nurse and report my grandmother's death so that our family could start the grieving process and that's what I did.

Not being there for your children, the death of a family member, the addiction of a family member, financial ruin, promiscuity no matter what you may be feeling guilty about, it's time to let it go. Don't act as though it never happened, don't ignore the consequences of your actions, but you have to stop letting it control your life. Today is the day that Guilt is notified of its last days in your house.

It may be hard for you to face these old feelings, to look those things you swept under the rug in the eye and that is why we do this with God and the Holy Spirit, our comforter. If this becomes hard for you, re-read the first chapter. Remind yourself of how good God is and how much He loves you.

LET'S PRAY

Most Gracious God,

Thank you for leading me this far. Thank you for courage. Please give me peace as I examine myself and my life. Help me face problems head on. Show me who and what can help me during this eviction.

Amen.

GROUNDS FOR EVICTION

Guilt is often welcomed by unconfessed sin. List 2 or 3 sins you are dealing with.

_____
_____
_____
_____
_____

How have the above sins and hiding from them impacted your life and brought on feelings of guilt.

_____
_____
_____
_____
_____

PREPARING FOR COURT

Go to God in prayer and confess your sins. Admit your weaknesses in those areas and ask for God's forgiveness and strength.

RE-ENFORCEMENTS: AFFIRMATIONS

Responsibility builds character, courage and comfort.

God gives me new mercies and grace each day.

My past mistakes do not determine my future.

RECESS: GUILT

Knowing what you are guilty of is the first step of overcoming guilt. When you have let go of the past and forgiven yourself, what can you do to avoid going back down the same path? Do you need to change your media intake? Social circle? Add devoted time for prayer to your schedule? End a relationship?

_____

_____

_____

_____

_____

_____

_____

_____

_____

_____

_____

_____

_____

_____

_____

_____

_____

_____

FOUR

SHAME

When I was 18 I had a best friend. We shared an apartment, a love of going out to clubs and multiple friends. We went to the same clubs on the same days every week and danced and laughed with the same people. We went to the mall together, to visit our families together and even worked together. There was no Laverne and Shirley in our circle, instead it was us.

Whenever things came up and we had to be separated, I couldn't make it a minute without someone asking me where she was. When she went places without me it was the same with her. It was almost annoying to the both of us. When we saw each other at home the first question asked was not "Did you have fun?" but "Who asked about me?" because we knew what the other person had been doing all night, explaining why we were out with different friends or even solo.

Guilt and Shame roll the same way, BFF's or Best Friends Forever. While guilt is the feeling of being responsible for a wrong doing, shame is the feeling of embarrassment or unworthiness associated with doing something wrong. Guilt may cause you to give money to your drug addict child while Shame will cause you to lie to your husband about it.

Guilt and Shame travel together because Guilt often makes you feel as though you can't tell anyone about your wrongdoings. Shame makes you feel unworthy, alone, that no one has ever done such a thing that you have. Shame causes you to live a bowed down life and willing to do anything to keep from being found out.

I grew up without a father. Growing up, Shame told me that made less than other children, especially because my mother had children by other men who were all in some form a part of their children's lives. I'll never forget the day a classmate and I were on our way to an oratorical contest. He was in 5th grade, myself in 3rd and this was my first year at a new school. He spoke "like a white person" which simply meant proper English. He dressed better than the kids at my school and we simply received him as better than us.

We were the only children in the school going so our parents had given permission for the teacher to transport us in her car. During our rehearsals we didn't have time to really get to know one another so along the ride he began to ask me what are considered regular questions. What school did I go to last year? Why do I go to this school now? Where do I live? How many siblings do I have? What does my mom do for a living? The bomb was dropped when he asked "What does your dad do for a living?"

I was just about paralyzed by this question. The only thing I knew about my dad was his name. That's it. Not what he looked like, where lived and I definitely didn't know what he did for a living.

Shame told me "Lie. Don't let him know that you don't know your dad." So I did. "He's a stockbroker." Where on Earth did I get that from? It is a little comical looking back at the situation. Me, a little black girl in one of the poorest neighborhoods in St. Louis, MO saying my dad is a stockbroker. For some reason I didn't want to lie and say a bus driver. I came up with a lie that I thought would flip the tables and make him feel small and put me on top.

The puzzled look on his face was just as comical. A fifth grader, he probably knew and understood the income and prestige that comes with being a stockbroker and was understandably confused as to how that was possible. He then asked "Where does he live?" As usual, one lie demands another. "In New York." I answered. "If he lives in New York then how did he meet your mom?" I was thankful at this time the teacher interjected with "Why don't you guys rehearse one more time before we get there."

Even though I had nothing to feel guilty about, seeing my siblings with their fathers made me feel as though there was something especially wrong with me to make my dad not come around. Guilt accused me of having done something that led to me being fatherless, shame made me feel unworthy because of it.

Just as with guilt, shame causes us to live subpar lives. Guilt comes as a result of sin, while Shame often causes us to sin. We lie, deceive and pretend to be someone we are not because Shame convinces us that our true selves are unworthy. When we live ashamed of things we have or haven't done it's as though we aren't believing in or accepting the forgiveness that Christ died for.

It is believed that there are two types of shame, Deserved and Undeserved. Deserved shame is something you feel when you are guilty of a wrong doing. As in, giving money to the drug addict family member. Undeserved shame is something you feel when you have done no wrong at all, such as me being ashamed for my father not being a part of my life. Deserved shame is the shame you would feel for getting caught stealing from the mall, Undeserved shame is the shame you would feel if you were out with your friend who got caught stealing and you had no idea.

Whether the Shame is deserved or undeserved, it has no right to occupy your mind. We know that deserved shame is simply conviction from God, to be dealt with in prayer and underserved shame is a trick of the enemy.
"For the kind of sorrow God wants us to experience leads us away from sin and results in salvation. There's no regret for that kind of sorrow. But worldly sorrow, which lacks repentance, results in spiritual death." 2 Corinthians 7:11 (NLT)

It is expected that when you are called out or when you call yourself out on things that you have done that a piece of you will be ashamed. We all want to see ourselves and be seen in the best light possible. However, that feeling is from God, urging you to come to Him with your issues. The point of it all is not to make you feel unworthy. When you go to God and let Him know that you don't like that feeling and asking for help to change then that is what you will get. When you try to hide from God and even yourself, you are living a lie which is essentially not living at all.

"The thief only comes to steal and kill and destroy." John 10:10 (ESV)

The thief here is the enemy. When I first read this as a teenager I thought it applied to material things and people's lives. Whenever anything bad would happen, we just said it was the enemy. If someone's car was stolen, job was lost or something of that magnitude, we blamed it on him. "That ain't nothing but the Devil!" was what we always said during bad times. However, as I got older I learned that the enemy is lot craftier than that. He comes to steal our peace of mind, kill our hopes and dreams and destroy our lives. The word says "does not come except to". That means that if he isn't stealing, killing or destroying he isn't around. That's his only purpose!

What a joy it is to know that Jesus is our shepherd, here to protect us and has given us the tools to fight Satan off. The enemy has already lost. He is already defeated. Victory is already ours. The enemy may come and convince us otherwise but this is what you must remember: The enemy can't beat us. He can't have our lives, he can't have our minds, and he can't have our souls. He can try convince us to give up the fight. He can try to convince us that Eviction Notice is a bunch of spiritual baloney, that Jesus can't defeat shame and that this is a lost cause. Do not give in! When shame takes over your life, there has to be a turning point and I thank God that's where you are.

During this eviction process, there will be people or even your own self-defeating thoughts that will try to throw you off, condemn you and maybe even ask how you could even utter the name of Jesus. Are you going to act like you forgot all that you have done? Since Guilt and Shame are BFF's the key to eradicating one applies to the other. Prayer and self-talk.

You have to have the courage to stand up to those thoughts and at least ignore the people posing the questions if you are not strong enough for confrontation. Talk back to those thoughts and eventually to those people!

"How can you even say the name Jesus?"

Simple, Jesus loves us. He GAVE His life for us and our sins! It wasn't taken or stolen but offered up willingly.

"Are you going to act like you forgot all that you have done?"

NO, but I don't have to let it take reign in my life.

We have to push toward the prize, a peace of mind. It had to be hard to conjure up the strength to go in front of her neighbors and ask forgiveness, especially if people lived then as they do today, like they have done no wrong. Admitting where you have fallen short will be tough, but know that on the side of that is forgiveness and peace. Once you have these things in your own life, it will be a joy to spread them into the lives of others.

LET'S PRAY

Father God,

Help me to understand that in you there is no shame. Help me to understand I am still loved. Help me to turn from sin and live in the safety of the shadow of your wings. Give me mentors and prayer partners to complete this eviction process and live in peace.

Amen.

GROUNDS FOR EVICTION

Name a time or situation that you have felt ashamed in your past. How did that affect your life? Was it Deserved or undeserved shame?

_____

_____

_____

_____

_____

What shameful situation are you dealing with now? How is it affecting your life? Is your current Shame Deserved or Undeserved?

_____

_____

_____

_____

_____

PREPARING FOR COURT

Write a simple, easy to remember prayer that speaks to your shame and re-enforces the forgiveness you have in Christ Jesus.

RE-ENFORCEMENTS: AFFIRMATIONS

Even when I stumble, I am unashamed.

In God there is only correction which is for my own good.

Releasing shameful things makes room for blessings.

RECESS: SHAME

How will you tell the difference between understanding you need to make a change and being ashamed? How can you make sure that you accept responsibility for your actions without being bogged down by shame?

_____

_____

_____

_____

_____

_____

_____

_____

_____

_____

_____

_____

_____

_____

_____

_____

_____

_____

FIVE

THE GANG'S ALL HERE

Imagine there's a parent who has to go out to town for business, a family emergency or a kid free vacation. There's a teenager who the parents decide can be trusted to not burn the house down and stay home, babysitter free. The teenager has been given permission for a friend or two to come over, order pizzas, watch a movie and go home. Friend one shows up with a 6 pack of beer and another guest. In the middle of a movie another friend shows up with a little marijuana, two more friends show up, hard liquor comes through and before you know it there's a full blown party complete with a keg, beer pong, people dancing on the roof and grandma's ashes in the middle of the living room floor! How did inviting friends over for movies and pizza turn a small fire, broken flat screen, stained carpet and more?

When Guilt and Shame come into your existence, they rarely and I mean rarely do so without inviting their friends to come hang around. Guilt and Shame are cowardly tenants. They don't want the blame for the damage they are causing and send someone else to take the blame. "She likes to stir the pot." The phrase means someone who likes to cause trouble, brings underlying issues to the surface often with bad intent. Several reality show stars have proven that some people like being known for stirring the pot. Guilt and Shame are not those people. I say they like to "stir the pot and drop the spoon".

They like to cause problems and then act like they had nothing to do with it. A person may lash out in anger and the anger gets all of the attention without bringing any focus to the root of the problem, the pot stirrer themselves, Guilt and Shame. Similar to gardening, if you don't attack your weeds by the root, the weeds will reappear. To identify who Guilt and Shame have living in your house, look at some of things that you do and you will find your answer.

When you feel guilty or ashamed about something do you lie about it? Do you go to desperate lengths to cover it up? Do you let other people take the blame? Deceit and/or Fear lives in your house.

When you feel guilty or ashamed do you take that frustration out on other people? Anger lives in your house.

When you feel guilty or ashamed do you ignore it, try to rationalize it or deny it all together? Pride lives in your house.

Ten times out of ten, Guilt and Shame invite other tenants in to destroy the character of your home. Ten times out of then, if you don't combat them they will win. These tenants lead to the faulty characters we become. They lead to liars, angry, prideful, jealous, boastful people. These character traits come to be because Guilt and Shame won't allow us to take responsibility for our actions or the next steps to living a peaceful life. Thank God He gives us strength to get these people gone and gone for good.

If you think you have a reason that validates any of these behaviors, you are being deceived. Someone may be thinking "My kids don't listen to me unless I get angry and yell." You may be thinking "Telling a little white lie here and there is what I have to do to be successful at work." There may be a few of you thinking "If I don't brag on what I know, I'll get overlooked at school and my grades will suffer." There is nothing that is of God that will require you to be angry, boastful or jealous. The enemy, through Guilt and Shame, may try to convince you that these are all true facts but you can choose to not believe him.   As a matter of fact, these behaviors are expressively spoken against.

FEAR

The Gang of Guilt and Shame include most often Fear. Fear is the 6'5" 300 pound friend of Guilt and Shame. Fear is their enforcer. Fear is who they call when you won't do what they say. Guilt and Shame may make the suggestions or even the rules for your life, while Fear is the one who looks at you menacingly that makes you tuck your tail and follow orders. Fear is the one who rationalizes what Guilt and Shame drop into your mindset. While Guilt and Shame may give the orders to the daily suicide we commit, Fear pulls the trigger. When Fear is not around, Guilt and Shame are much less powerful and that is why they hardly go anywhere without it.

Here is a journal entry from October 7, 2013 when I was going through my eviction process. I didn't know it then, but my addiction to the approval of others was based on fear of abandonment which came from guilt and shame. The feelings I had as a 28 year old woman dated back to things that happened when I was 3.

"When I am criticized, I feel low. It feels like I have taken a serious blow to the stomach. Inside I feel like I have crouched over, my insides feel like they have been crumpled up like last week's grocery list. I then feel angry, bitter, disappointed in myself and want to go ball up in my bed. What I would like to do at all costs is avoid it and do everything perfectly so that criticism doesn't happen. I know that isn't a possibility."

Fear is synonymous with panic. We all know that the first rule of survival in an emergency is "DON'T PANIC." Why? Because under panic we don't think, we simply accept that doom is eminent. When Guilt and Shame place thoughts of doubt and insignificance in our minds, we don't think about how irrational it is, out of fear, we accept that they must be right. In my personal experience living with guilt, shame and fear forced me into an addiction. Though I turned to drugs and alcohol many, many times before my eviction process began, that's not the addiction that did the most damage. I was addicted to approval.

Between the ages of 3 and 12 I was regularly molested by mother's boyfriend. I never felt any guilt about being molested. I know that there was nothing I could have done to prevent the initial or subsequent episodes. I did feel ashamed and even worthless because I didn't speak up about it. As an adult, I ended up in therapy.

One day my therapist asked me to imagine myself as 3 year old Erica, young and free and then she would help me to live my life from that space of freedom. It was hard for me to admit, that I couldn't imagine being free. Abuse and fear had been a constant part of my life from almost the beginning. I was scared to be alone with my abuser, I was scared when I saw him walking down the street, I was scared when I saw him beat my mom. It was the shame of it all that crippled me.

As a result, my sisters were removed from the home and to an extent ostracized by my mother. I was about 5 or 6 when this happened and because I didn't want to be rejected by mother, I never said "Hey, me too!" I think because I was so young people assumed he didn't bother, but that's not true. I didn't feel bad because of what was happening to me, but I felt bad because my sisters felt bad. They would come over for visits and we would have to pretend not to be home because the only way they could visit was IF the abuser wasn't there and most times he was.

I became exasperated with the situation and wanted to go live with my grandmother but I felt ashamed that I hadn't spoken up earlier and having to live with my abuser was my punishment. Fear told me that if I told or even resisted the late night visits, my mother would send me away but to where since my grandmother wouldn't want me? I figured it would be best to just do what I was told and stay out of the way. This is how my addiction to approval was born.

I tried my very best to be perfect. I wasn't perfect my any means but that was my goal. I did whatever my mom asked, as any child should, but it wasn't out of respect, I was scared that she would dispose of me. As an adult looking back, I know that this was a completely irrational thought.

As a child these things weren't explained to me and I was forced to draw my own conclusions. Based on what I gathered I figured that in order to stay at home with my mom, I needed to try my hardest to be good and not mention the abuse. My mother's boyfriend abused her in many ways. He had made her weak and isolated her from our family. I became her right hand and I didn't want to let her down. My mind told me that I couldn't let her down. Having my mom come home and be pleased with what I had done became my only option and that's what I strived for each and every day.

By the time I was 8 I was her commander in chief. I changed diapers, made bottles and sometimes cooked hot dog dinners. I wasn't lonely and I didn't feel like I was missing out on anything because taking care of home was all I knew. Naturally I felt more responsible than other kids and took it upon myself to be in charge. Needless to say this didn't work out too well with my peers. I had problems with other kids telling me "You think you know everything." And it didn't help that I did. I always raised my hand in class and I was a teacher's pet because that's what worked at home. I would volunteer to take attendance, always raised my hand to answer questions and whatever else it took to be recognized. I didn't want the attention, I wanted the "Good job Erica!"

Eventually I learned that if I wanted to be accepted at school and make friends, I couldn't boss everyone around rather I had to do whatever they said. If I was ever asked my opinion, my answer would always be "It doesn't matter." I couldn't tell you what I wanted to eat, where I wanted to go, by the time I became an adult I couldn't decide which route to take the store without consulting the other passengers and going the way they thought was best. It was a terrible way to live because the addiction was two-fold. On one side came the high from being approved and other side came the depression from being rejected.

Whenever I was criticized or rejected it was a crushing blow to my self-esteem. It wasn't the normal embarrassment a person might feel. I literally felt like I could just die if someone wasn't pleased with the way I had done something. Once, when I was 13 or 14 I attempted suicide because my mother yelled at me about not cleaning the kitchen right. Guilt and Shame told me that death was the better option. I held back tears as I went up the stairs to my bedroom, embarrassed that I, the ring leader of the house, had done something wrong. I took a belt and tightened it around my neck and pulled as hard as I could until my arms hurt. I realized I needed to hang it from something on the ceiling and looked up. All that was there was a globe light fixture and I knew it wouldn't work. This began my transition from depression to anger and back to depression. The battle of the two lasted much into my adulthood, until my eviction.

DECEIT

Guilt and Shame most often convince us to cover our tracks. They make us feel as though anything we have done or not done is something to be hidden away, never to be seen by the light of day. The easiest way to cover something up is to lie about it. It works remarkably well, especially in situations where you have earned someone's trust. It's sad though because most times a lie never ends. If you lie once, you'll eventually have to lie twice. The old saying goes "One good lie deserves another." Truthfully speaking "One good lie REQUIRES another." Before you know it you have created a web of lies that will eventually cause you to doubt what your own name is.

If you are thinking that lying is your default setting and a part of your framework, you have hope in God.
"Do not lie to one another since you have put off the old man with his deeds and have put on the new man who is renewed in knowledge to the image of Him who created you." Colossians 3:9 (NKJV)

Once you have put Liar out of your house, you can be free to tell the truth because he doesn't live there anymore. Liar can be replaced with Peace and Goodness because they will in the new group of tenants you move into your house. Peace and Goodness come with the renewal, with the remodeling that God will do to you with this eviction process because He desires us to be like Him since He is who made us.

ANGER

Ephesians is one of my favorite books of The Bible. It's full of practical instruction and wisdom that was instrumental in my eviction process. As I was nearing the start of my eviction I had become defiantly angry. I was angry that I had been used for most of my life, I was angry about the job I had, I was angry that multiple friendships and relationships had failed and frankly I was angry at God. One morning, while working at the job that made me angry, I sat in a waiting room reading a small bible that had been given to me as a gift. A gentleman told me to turn to Ephesians 6:13 and it changed my life right then and there (more on that later).

"Let all bitterness, wrath, anger, clamor and evil speaking be put away from you, with all malice. And be kind to one another, tenderhearted, forgiving one another, even as God in Christ forgave you." Ephesians 4:31-32 (NKJV)

Reading that let me know that my anger, my wrath had no place in me. All of the things that I was mad about were forgivable in the same way that my sins are. If I wanted to be forgiven then I could not hang on to the pointless anger inside of me. Remaining angry is like saying that whatever issue you have is too big for God to resolve. When the anger is let go, then the Guilt and Shame have no enforcer to push you into their trap.

If you think that the person you are holding anger against should be held responsible for their pain against you, you are wrong. Just as Guilt and Shame have an impact on your life, they have an impact in the lives of others. Yes, as people all things we do have to be decided on and then we have to be committed to carry out the actions. Nothing is really done without thought. When a person hurts you it's hard to accept that it may have been intentional. The bigger picture in that is to realize that we all have internal wars we are fighting and they simply have lost the battle during that particular time.

Instead of holding on to your anger for that person specifically, it's best to present the spiritual forces at work in their lives to God for Him to deal with.

"For we do not wrestle against flesh and blood, but against principalities, against powers, against the rulers of the darkness of this age, against spiritual hosts of wickedness in the heavenly places"   Ephesians 6:12 (NKJV)

Let the anger go. It's not them, it's something bigger than them going on. Let God handle it. It's what He's here for.

Am I asking you to never get angry again? No, of course not. Being angry is a natural feeling and sometimes can anger can be quite the motivator. Sometimes anger can motivate us to do the wrong thing. If you make a bad grade on a test or a huge mistake at work and your anger motivates you to work harder and smarter, that's a good thing. If you make a bad grade or a mistake at work and your anger motivates you to assault your teacher or supervisor, then that's bad.

Under the influence of anger, it's easy to say mean things to someone, to physically hurt them or even come up with a plan to hurt, harm or embarrass them. None of these things will do anything to ease your pain. As a matter of fact, the enemy we are fighting will tempt you into doing these things then leave you feeling guilty or ashamed about how you handled yourself. Talk about a two-edged sword!

"If you become angry, do not let your anger lead you into sin, and do not stay angry all day. Don't give the Devil a chance." Ephesians 4:26-27 (GNT)

It's ok to be angry, but we have to be careful not to hold onto it or sin as a result of it.

PRIDE

Let's get one thing straight. If you get an A on a report, make the varsity squad, get the promotion you've worked hard for or simply get all of the laundry done for once, I do not want you to not take pride in your accomplishments. If you have a presentation to do, a child to raise or a department to run, I don't want you to not take pride in your task and give a half effort. There is a difference between taking pride and being proud.

Pride is a feeling or deep pleasure or satisfaction derived from one's own achievements, the achievements of those with whom one is closely associated, or from qualities or possessions that are widely admired. Words synonymous with pride are joy, pleasure, please, happy.

Proud is defined as having or showing a high or excessively high opinion of oneself or one's importance or having or showing a consciousness of one's own dignity. To clarify, you can take pride in your appearance therefore making sure you look presentable and clean every day. You can be proud about the fact that you need help paying your electric bill, refusing to ask for help and forced to live in darkness once the power is disconnected.

"When pride comes, then disgrace but with the humble is wisdom." Proverbs 11:2 (ESV)

The same as anger, when pride comes into the picture it's as though saying your problems are too big for God. Humbling yourself to God simply means going to Him in prayer and asking for help while admitting that the problem is too big for you. Trust me, it's what He wants you to do. God doesn't give us trials to laugh and poke fun at us as we scrape and struggle. He allows us tests to keep us dependent on Him because after all, once we ask for help He makes it available for us. Being proud is only damaging to us. We may think that not asking for help, either from God or others, is teaching them a lesson or teaching them that we don't need anybody but it only hurts us in the end.

Take the story of the lost son (Luke 15:11-32). In the story there's a rich man who has two sons. As was the order of things, they were promised a nice inheritance upon the death of him. The younger of the two asked if they could have their inheritances early, right then and there.

The father agreed and soon after the younger son left the family home. He went to a faraway country and spent the money and had the time of his life. Soon there was a famine in the country and because he was an outsider (and probably didn't have a good attitude towards others spending all that money), no one would help him at all. Eventually, he decided to become a citizen of that country so that he could a job and the only one he could find was a pig feeder. He still couldn't afford to eat and would have gladly ate the food that the pigs ate if he had been allowed to.

Why didn't he go home as soon as the money ran out? I can imagine that he felt guilty for convincing his father to give him that money, shamed that he had spent it on fast living and then became too proud to admit that to his father that he had made a mistake. Because of that pride, he went from the son of a wealthy man who had no wants to being a starving pig feeder in a faraway land. Guilt and Shame probably convinced him that his father and brother would have nothing to do with him so he tried to make do on his own.

Eventually, probably on the brink of death, he realized that he sinned against God and His father during his party time and figured he would humble himself, go home and ask his father for a job there. After all, his father's servants have enough food to eat and spare. He had become so desolate, so desperate that he finally had no choice but to go home. To his surprise his father not only accepted him, but had a great party for him because he had been waiting for him to come home.

Guilt and Shame will have you thinking that you have committed the unthinkable and all the while God is waiting on you.

LET'S PRAY

Dear Lord,

Help me to notice other tenants in my house. Continue to be my strength during this eviction process. Take from me all seeds of sin including selfishness, deceit, illicit gain, anger, wrath and bitterness from yesterday. Increase my humility, strength and hunger for you.

Amen

GROUNDS FOR EVICTION

Who, if any, is the biggest accomplice of Guilt and Shame living in your house? You may choose from the list or write your own.

Fear Jealousy   Deceit   Anger   Wrath
Depression Bitterness   Low Self Esteem   Pride Ego

_____

_____

_____

_____

Which of the Fruits of The Spirit can help you drive out these tenants and how?

_____

_____

_____

_____

_____

PREPARING FOR COURT

Write a simple prayer asking God to help you see yourself clearly.

RE-ENFORCEMENTS: AFFIRMATION

I control my property and who lives in my house.

I will rise above _____ (list "tenant" here.)

Honesty is better than denial.

RECESS: THE GANG'S ALL HERE

How does it feel knowing that guilt and shame have brought subtenants into your life? How do your subtenants show up in your life? What thoughts and actions can you be on alert for to let you know that guilt and shame are stirring the pot?

_____

_____

_____

_____

_____

_____

_____

_____

_____

_____

_____

_____

_____

_____

_____

SIX

VIOLATIONS

When you imagined your dream home, did you imagine tenants such as Guilt and Shame living there? Of course not, that's not who God designed us to be. It's amazing that so many of us deal with them and their issues. Most times these issues go unnoticed and eventually we begin to think they are normal. I know I did. I have shared with you what the word of God says about Guilt, Shame and their comrades and have even shared some specific examples from life. I pray that you have been able to relate to them. This chapter will explore some common thought patterns that are often Guilt and Shame induced.

The theory here is that Guilt and Shame are ruining your house which is your mind. That's why it's important that we look at common thoughts, to expose them and take them to the judge during our application for eviction. These violations and many more are the grounds that we have to evict Guilt and Shame. After all, the violations are what make the case. The sub-tenants themselves are grounds for eviction but I want to take you a little deeper so that we know just where they may have come from.

I believe that when something happens in our lives we can have one of three train of thought about it:

What the enemy plants

What we want to do

What God wants us to do.

Because the enemy normally comes in screaming, these thoughts are normally our first. I think it would be fair to say that when someone offends us, our first thought it to offend them. If someone physically hurts us, our knee jerk reaction is to hit them back. Those are the thoughts of the enemy. The thoughts that, if followed through will have us deep in the murky waters of sin or even on the 10:00 news.

Our own thoughts are sometimes a step towards rational yet still carnal. These are the thoughts that tell us that we will still get them back, but not in public. They tell us we CAN get them and they DESERVE it. They may even tell us to let the other person get away with is THIS TIME but that if it should so happen again, it's going down.

Our God thoughts normally come last. I say this because we have to seek Him. We have to fight off those devilish and carnal thoughts often come. The powerful thing about God thoughts is that they come through as a powerful yet faint whisper. The good thing is that eventually we will know better and keep our mental station tuned to Holy 118.9.

I have shared with you some exhibits from my case and I'm sure you have exhibits of your own. Did you know that there is a name for the times when you feel like you may as well not even try? Hint, it's not depression. It's these types of thoughts that snowball and land you in that terrible space and it's completely avoidable.

The key to overcoming Guilt and Shame is to change your mind. Period. Just as we have to confront Guilt and Shame before we can move them out, we have to confront what they have been making us think so that we can see how irrational it is. As long as we are living under the reign of Guilt and Shame, we won't see anything wrong with these things.

I can tell you several examples of the Guilt and Shame led thoughts that turned to decisions that led to me being on the brink of suicide. Sure, it will give God glory because He not only kept me from doing it but delivered me from that spirit. I used to crave death like you crave chocolate. I would speed through yellow lights and run red lights in hopes of a terrible accident. I drank myself into stupors, started several bar fights and even did drugs. I wanted to die in some tragic accident but God favored me.

I remember in detail the accident that sped up the change in my life. I had went to see a guy friend and was rushing home. It was raining and dark. I had about a 30 minute drive and I set the cruise control to 50mph. I didn't know that was a no-no. I was driving on 55-North through downtown St. Louis and had just taken the exit that goes smoothly onto 70-West. There is a sharp right turn there and I had just got a text. I looked at the road, looked down to get my phone and dropped it in a cup of wine. I know, I was tripping. I gasped at dropping my phone in the wine and thinking about how I would still drink it when, BAM!

I smacked the median wall on the right side. This sent the car spinning around and hitting the front against the left side median wall which sent the car into another spin hitting the back against the same wall. I ended up sitting horizontally across two lanes of traffic and by the time I realized what had happened, I wanted to hurry up and get out the way before other cars came around the curve. When I looked out of the window, all of the cars were at a standstill, they weren't even trying to pass.

If I shouldn't have died from the impact of hitting a wall 3 times, then one of those cars definitely should've hit me and killed me. God didn't see fit for that to happen. I heard him say "Ok, you've had your accident. Now what?" After the initial shock of being in a terrible accident had worn off, I realized that not only was the car ok but so was I. Not a scratch on me.

Why in the world would I have thought that if I died it would make my life easier? It was an attack fueled by the enemy and these are often the types of attacks he uses to send us spiraling out of control.

I referenced before that the enemy comes only to steal, kill and destroy. He can see the spiritual realm that we cannot. Even though he chooses not to serve Him, the enemy knows just how great our God is. He doesn't want you to think that your house is something worth stealing, killing or destroying but it is. If it wasn't, if God had nothing for you, the enemy would leave you alone. The more you feel his attacks, the more he is trying to keep you from. It's important that we recognize that so that we may put a stop to it. That's why it's said that recognizing that there is a problem is the first step. If you don't think anything is wrong then you won't try to fix it!

I'm going to use the example of losing a basketball game and being looked over at school/work to explain these situations. In sports and school/work alike we all have some relation to. Those of you who have never played sports have all been to school/work. Those of you who have never been to school/work have probably played a pick-up game. If neither of the scenarios appeal to you then you are free to think about your life and take an inventory on if you have had any of these types of thoughts. The thought processes are very similar, but can be different in each person. When you think of the sub-tenants in your house, most of them stem from one or more of these thought processes.

As you read, highlight or circle the thought patterns that are most prevalent in your life.

OVERGENERALIZATION

This happens when you see a single negative event as a never ending pattern. In the instance of losing a basketball game a player may have thoughts like "We will never have a winning season." "If we keep playing like this I won't get a scholarship, I won't go to college and I'll end up working a dead end job." If your idea at work is put on the shelf or you answer a question incorrectly during class you may think "I won't ever get a promotion/graduate at this rate." That's over generalization.

What makes a thought an overgeneralization is when it goes too far, when it tries to connect extremes that have nothing to do with each other. While thinking, "If I don't make this shot we may lose the game", is rational, thinking if you miss a shot that your entire career is over is not.

When we over generalize, it's normally out of being ashamed and inviting to Fear.

MENTAL FILTER

This is when we pick out a single negative detail and focus only on that. If the star player on the losing team of a basketball game scores 28 points but thinks only about the 7 shots he missed he is thinking with a mental filter on. When you focus only on the fact that your idea was shelved this week, ignoring the fact that a different idea was used last week, that's thinking with your mental filter on.

While wanting to assess your performance and think about ways to improve is completely healthy, it takes a wrong turn when you can only think about the negative. It's important to look at the complete picture and focus on the positives. That way your actions are based on, "What I can do more of?" which is typically easier because you have already proven what you know how to do.

Thinking with a mental filter can be from Guilt or Shame and is inviting to Anger and Fear.

JUMPING TO CONCLUSIONS

This is when you try to be a mind reader. This is when you are so scared of something happening that you try to prevent it from happening. Sometimes you may even go about your day as if that prediction has already come true. Such as losing a ball game one week and not even trying in practice because "we'll just lose anyway." This is when you feel like since your last idea was shut down that you won't say anything at the meetings since "my idea will just be shut down anyway".

This is when you decide on your own that someone doesn't like you or is upset with you and you don't even bother to ask. You go around avoiding them or initiating mean words because, although unfounded, you already know they don't like you.

Jumping to conclusions is a dangerous thought process to have because it keeps you from living in the real world, let alone the moment. It's constant turmoil because none of us can predict the future or how a person might react. We spend so much time preparing for when a situation might happen, that life passes us by.

Jumping to conclusions is inviting to Anger, Fear and Pride.

EMOTIONAL REASONING

This is when you assume that your negative thoughts are indicative of the reality of things. It's like saying "Since I feel this way, then it must be true." If the star player starts to feel like he is a loser, then he plays like one.

So many times in movies we hear therapists says "Say something starting with the phrase "I feel" and that may be one of the reasons that people think that because they feel something, it's true. We are all entitled to our opinions, but our feelings require processing. A feeling can only come from a thought and face it, we can be wrong! If we can think the wrong things then we can feel the wrong things! Our feelings, like our thoughts are to be tested not trusted. Our minds can play tricks on us and when they do, we have to direct our minds to God.

Using emotional reasoning can lead to Fear and Deceit. I say deceit because we don't want to be exposed honestly. We don't want anyone to know when or how they have hurt us so when we have these irrational thoughts and feelings it's easy for us to lie and cover them up.

SHOULD STATEMENTS

This is when you try to motivate yourself with should and shouldn't statements. "I should've made those baskets last week so I'm not going to hang out with my friends this week, I'll practice instead", is what the ball player would say. Contrarily, when we direct should and shouldn't statements at other people is when we feel anger, resentment or frustration with them. "My teammates should've made their baskets too!"

Should statements are probably the most rampant. I hear this so much in daily conversation and it takes a lot of restraint for me to not go into a deeper conversation with it.

"She should have done this!" or "He should've done that!" is a statement that makes my skin crawl now that I know where it stems from.

When we make a "should" statement, it's normally because we think that if we had or hadn't done something then the situation would have turned out more favorable for us and that leads into jumping to conclusions.

These are just a few of the violations that Guilt and Shame were guilty of in my property. They are different but so deeply intertwined. One can lead to another and another and before you know it, you don't know left from right.

These processes had me thinking that everything was my fault and that I should have done better, that people didn't like me and that there was no point in even trying. Is it easy to see how I ended up in a depression?

One of the tools I used to get out it was writing. Not this book, this has come several (well, about 3) years later. When I was in the throng of it and fighting for my life, I started to test my feelings. I would write down the thoughts I was having and then come up with a counter thought/plan to beat it. Here is an example:

I don't want strife. Instead I choose peace. I don't want depression. Instead I choose happiness. I don't want my happiness dependent on someone else. Instead I choose to make my own happiness. I don't want a dirty house. Instead I choose to clean my house. I don't want to feel confused. Instead I choose to accept how I really feel. I don't want to predict the future. Instead I choose to enjoy the now. I don't want to gain weight. Instead I choose to be active. I don't want to lose my job. Instead I choose to work hard. I don't want to compare my life to others. Instead I choose to love my own.

Writing your thoughts and counter thoughts out is not a magic spell that makes these things happen. All this does is help you see the negative, Guilt and Shame induced thoughts and help you to generate your list of violations. Honestly speaking, I still have problems keeping my house spic and span but I don't feel guilty about it anymore.

I'm a single mom which means my son, although he sees his dad regularly, lives with me. That means that all responsibility falls exclusively on me. I'm also writing a book while working 40+ hours a week so if a load of dishes gets put off until tomorrow then I'm okay with that.

When a thought is formed in your mind, before giving it room to become a feeling that is acted upon, ask yourself if it is from the enemy, from yourself or from God. If you can't distinguish between the three, then find something to be thankful for in spite of the situation. It's important that going forward you choose to think thankful thoughts. These thought patterns all focus on negative things, both factual and imagined. To negate these things, think thankful thoughts. If you lose a basketball game, be thankful that you have the use of your limbs. You do know that there are some people who can't use their legs don't you?

Be thankful that you have good lungs. There are people who can't sit up in bed and do nothing without the assistance of oxygen. If you are able to not just run up and down a basketball court but breathe while doing it then a simple loss shouldn't matter. Even if you're in the NBA and lose a game, there is still tomorrow. Even in loss of games, friendships, jobs and more you can still be hopeful on purpose. You can still have positive expectation that a good thing will happen. Thinking like this will eliminate the thought processes of Guilt and Shame.

LET'S PRAY

Father and God,

Thank you for helping me to plainly see my violations. I know these are not a result of your fruit. In school, work, sports and relationships, let me be trusting of you. Show me what inner peace looks like and lead me to that path.

Amen

GROUNDS FOR EVICTION

Which thought patterns have you had before? Which of the thought patterns are most prevalent in your life?

_____

_____

_____

_____

_____

In realizing what thought patterns you use, what counteractions can you use to stop them?

Example: Instead of jumping to conclusions I will make fully informed decisions.

_____

_____

_____

_____

_____

PREPARING FOR COURT

Write or say a simple prayer asking God to give you a mind at ease and to increase your trust in Him.

RE-ENFORCEMENTS: AFFIRMATIONS

When I think positively, positive things happen.

I have the power to control my thoughts.

Positive thoughts produce positive outcomes.

RECESS: VIOLATIONS

What would you do if you knew you couldn't fail? Big thinking cannot happen in the presence of violators. Use this space to describe the life that awaits you with your new thinking processes.

_____

_____

_____

_____

_____

_____

_____

_____

_____

_____

_____

_____

_____

_____

_____

_____

_____

_____

SEVEN

YOU'VE BEEN SERVED

Today is the day we notify Guilt and Shame that it's about to go down.

We have identified the tenants and sub tenants we want to evict as well as their violations. I can imagine you being all wound up because you had no idea that Guilt and Shame were behind some of the schemes going on in your life. You want them gone and gone yesterday. That's good and I need you to use that energy to serve them with the subpoena for court. Some of you may go back and forth and the time is now to choose peace.

You may have questions of doubt and fear. You may wonder what your life will be like without your old buddies and pals. That is ok and completely normal. We will deal with what you say to them soon and very soon.

Right now, before you read another word, you have to make up your mind to change your mind. This is it, Guilt and Shame will be served of your intentions to kick them to the curb. In this moment, you have to decide that no matter what may come or how the chips may fall that living with these tenants has not been good for you.

By making up your mind to change your mind, you will be shaking things up. Eventually you will begin to say no to people to which the answer has always been yes or vice versa. In my experience, I began to assert myself and my decisions, not letting them depend on what other people wanted me to do.

This was very scary and particularly nerve wrecking. Don't look at it that way. Don't think of this as something that will flip your life upside down. It may, but it will only be the shifting that occurs when you start to trust God.

The miracle will be what you have left after the shaking so please don't be fearful about this! When you look at something negatively, that's what it will become. You should look at this as a decision to love yourself because that's what it is. Just as loving another person should be unchanging, so should loving yourself. In making up your mind to change your mind, you should also be making up your mind to love yourself and NOT changing your mind about it.

Doubt and fear may cause you to wonder how you will do such a thing. I implore you, don't give in. When you accept responsibility for your actions and the forgiveness provided by Jesus Christ, you are a new creature. The old things that you did don't matter and neither do the thoughts or people that will throw them in your face. Having a sordid past does not disqualify you from the kingdom of Heaven. There are many instances in the bible of Jesus ignoring the self-righteous or "church folk" as we call them and going to the most desperate person in the crowd. There are many times that God takes the most unlikely candidate for a job and uses him or her in an unimaginable way.

Take Moses for example. We all know him. The "let my people go", parted the Red Sea, announced the 10 commandments Moses. He was an orphan, in jeopardy of being executed as a toddler per orders of Pharaoh. His mom put him in a basket and set him afloat on the Nile River in hopes of him surviving. He ends up being found by Pharaoh's daughter who his mom works for! So even though he was technically abandoned, he still grew up in the arms of his mom. Living as the son of Pharaoh's daughter basically made him Pharaoh's grandson. Even though I'm sure he had everything he could possibly want and need at his disposal, he still felt out of place.

Something inside of him lets him know that he is more Hebrew, who are slaves, than Egyptian which is what he is being raised as. One day he sees and Egyptian man fighting with a Hebrew man. He kills the Egyptian man and hides his body. The next day he saw the Hebrew man from the day before fighting another Hebrew. He asked them why they are fighting, they are brothers. The Hebrew man is offended and says "Who are you to judge us? What are you going to do? Kill me like you killed the Egyptian yesterday?"

Moses fled. The guilt from having committed a murder took over him and out of fear of being found out, he ran, like most of us do. He ends up living in the meadows and being a shepherd. Imagine this, going from a life of grandeur, in a palace with servants, to being a shepherd! Moses had people ready to wait on him, hand and foot. He went from that to working long hours standing in the sun, in the middle of nowhere, watching sheep.

I'm not sure what would have happened if Moses had stayed and faced his punishment but guilt made him go from bad (feeling out of place) to possibly worse. Moses was fine living his mediocre life until God called him to be greater. God told Moses to go back to Pharaoh and demand that the Hebrews be delivered from bondage. Moses protested, he had become comfortable being a shepherd living with his in-laws, wife and children. He even tried to tell God no and to go find someone else because He had a stutter, he wasn't eloquent.

However, when God has something planned for your life not even you can stop it. Look at Moses, a guilt ridden murderer who can barely speak and God not only forgave him but used him to free a whole nation. (See Exodus Chapters 1-4)

Are you thinking that's just a happenstance? Take the story of Paul. Paul was a hired murderer of Christians. When Christianity began to spread, Paul was hired to go and kill as many Christians as he could and he was good at it too! This man, who didn't even believe in God, was met by Jesus, forgiven and used to start several churches and write most of The New Testament.

When Jesus died on the cross for us, He died for all of us and all of our sins. Accepting that forgiveness and going forward to live a better life is yours for the taking. 2 Corinthians 5:17 says "Therefore, if anyone is in Christ, he is a new creation; old things have passed away; behold all things have become new."

Now that your mind has been made up to live free of guilt and shame, that guilt and shame ridden life of yours is dead. You have a new life in Christ full of purpose and joy, if you only believe it. Dead is the life where you are timid, bowed down and taken advantage of, and alive is a life full of the fruit of the spirit.

Accepting the forgiveness of Jesus Christ is only half of this step. The second half is forgiving others. You may be holding on to some grudges from your past or even your current state that may or may not contribute to the guilt or shame you feel at this time. No matter what, you have to forgive the people who have hurt you in order to receive the forgiveness of Jesus Christ. It feels so good knowing that Jesus died for our sins but sometimes we have a hard time accepting the fact that He died for the sins of those who have hurt us as well.

Jesus tells us time and time again that whatever we want from Him, we have to give it to others. "Judge not lest ye be judged." "Forgive others as I have forgiven you." "Blessed are the merciful for they will receive mercy." It's a two way street.

What's the most horrible crime you can think of? Based on internet comments, I bet a lot you are thinking harming children, more specifically being a pedophile. I agree. I've always heard that molesting a child "takes away their innocence."

I didn't know what that meant until I was about 25. If a man takes away a little girls innocence, it's evidenced by the fact that she doesn't feel comfortable hugging her uncles. She tenses when her basketball coach walks behind her to help her with her free throw form. She doesn't accept invitations to sleep overs and slumber parties for fear of a man being in the house. I know because these are all things I felt growing up.

I'm not sure how long my mother was in the relationship with her new boyfriend before the abuse started. It lasted until the very end. I know that he abused my mother, physically and financially, which is probably why she stayed with him once he was exposed. I know that my mother had us sleep in our clothes in efforts to thwart his actions but it didn't help.

My mother was ordered to end the relationship with this man but she did not. The relationship continued and so did the abuse. I became so used to it, I even asked this man if I could call him "Daddy". Eventually my mother became strong enough to end the relationship, about 10 years later. I was in the 6th grade. The innocence that I lost has never been seen again, but there was plenty of resentment and anger once I was finally old enough to understand that my childhood wasn't normal.

I got along ok with my mother and hated this man. It wasn't until I began my eviction process that I realized I carried unforgiveness for not just this man but my mom as well. With the help of The Holy Spirit, I was able to empathize with my mother and even my abuser. I realized that if my mom could have done better, she would have. I can't imagine any parent being ok with their child being hurt in any way, OR, feeling like there's nothing they can do to help.

The mother I have now is one of the strongest women I know. If this woman was around in the late 80's- early 90's I'm sure things would have turned out different. I can't help but to assume that the same tenants who crippled me, crippled my mom when the announcement that her boyfriend was molesting her daughters was made. After realizing these things I made the decision to show my mom that I love her. I know she knew that I loved her but I realized that she also knew what she did wrong. I didn't want to drag her into a conversation about the past that she didn't want to have but for me, it had to be done.

During the poking and question asking I did during my eviction process, it was said that my abuser may have been abused himself. Does that make it right? Of course not. Did that help me to understand what his mind set may have been? Yes. What if he wasn't abused? I believe that an adult attracted to children has a mental illness, a sickness that needs psychological attention and intense therapy. If my abuser was not abused as a child and is mentally ill, why would I hold on to anger and unforgiveness for him? It was something he couldn't, or at least thought he couldn't, help.

I don't know if these opinions of mine sound irrational or not, but these are the questions I have asked myself to help me forgive. When trying to forgive someone for a grave wrong, it's best to try to understand who they were in that moment.

It's not easy and it may not always make the most sense, but making sense out of it is not your job. Your job is to forgive and not hold it against that person. You don't have to forget, you don't have to tell them "It's ok" especially if it's not.

People often confuse forgiveness with permission and that's why it's easier to hold a grudge. We feel a sense of power in being mad, showing them that they don't have permission to hurt us. Forgiveness is not saying "Hey, I enjoy being hurt like that. Do it again anytime." Forgiveness is saying "Whether or not you meant to hurt me is not what I'm looking into. I was hurt. Period. However, Jesus forgives you for hurting me and so do I."

Would it have been easier for me to act as though these things didn't happen? Would it have been easier to be nice on the surface but full of discontent on the inside? It would have been easier in the short term because I wouldn't have had to revisit those sore spots. I wouldn't have had to remember the smells, the songs and how I felt in those dark moments.

If you think that because you choose to act as though something didn't happen, that's not forgiveness. If you go around acting like things didn't happen, putting them in the back of your mind, that's doing yourself a disservice. You can't proclaim to God that you want to be a new creature but still wear your old clothes.

You may be thinking that you can go on not forgiving the wounds and people of your past and you can, but you will be the only one who feels the pain of that. Thinking like that is similar to drinking poison and expecting the other person to die.

Thinking like that is like putting yourself in a permanent prison. Not forgiving neutralizes your own growth potential. It gives way for death to your dreams, hopes and your heart. Think about that for a moment. All forgiving other people does is open the door for you to be forgiven as well. Forgiveness is not opening the door to a relationship with that person. Forgiveness is not acting as though the hurt never happened. Unforgiveness is like drinking poison and expecting the other person to die. All forgiving other people does is open the door for you to be forgiven as well.

Forgiveness is a big idea because naturally we want to hurt those who hurt us. It's immediate and in our flesh and ego, we are always right or in my opinion, the victim. In forgiveness, we have to make a decision to forgive and then keep forgiving every time we think about the situation, no matter how we feel, instead of mulling in those feelings. In forgiveness we have to realize and convince ourselves that people aren't out to get us. If someone is in fact out to get you then that is their problem and not yours. Going against the natural grain of the fiber of our being is a hard thing. On our own, we are not strong enough to do this. The Lord can change us and He is willing to help us be more like Him.

Loving our enemies or those who have hurt us is exceptional in God's eyes. People often say "I'm a good person", because they are nice to people who are nice to them. Let that same person's schoolyard bully walk in the room and watch that "good person" show ugliness you didn't know they had.

In God's eyes, being good and loving on those who can are good to us and loving on those who can repay us is no good. It's easy, it's simple and it is something that we can do in our own human nature. Looking past a person's faults as He does with us is where we give Him glory.

God has great plans for us, bigger than we can imagine or think. You have made up your mind to change your mind. You are serving Guilt and Shame with an eviction notice today because you want to step into what God has for you. You know that God has a purpose for you and your life but, I tell you this, He can't use us with a bitter heart.

LET'S PRAY

Heavenly Father,

Thank you for forgiveness. Each day is a new chance to get things right and today I take advantage of that. I can forgive because you forgive. Help me to realize that forgiving others does not give them a pass in my life, but gives me a pass to receive all you have for me.

Amen

GROUNDS FOR EVICTION

Who are you holding unforgiveness for and why?

_____

_____

_____

_____

_____

Imagine if Jesus told you could hurt the person who hurt you if you had never sinned before. Would you be able to do it or would your past sins put you in the same need of forgiveness?

_____

_____

_____

_____

_____

PREPARATION FOR COURT

Write and recite a simple prayer asking God how to forgive yourself or others for things of the past.

RE-ENFORCEMENTS: AFFIRMATIONS

I forgive _____.

I release the hurt and anger of my past.

I love myself more than I hate _____.

RECESS: YOU'VE BEEN SERVED

Forgiving people who have hurt you benefits you more than them. Do you believe that to be true? If so, explain and if not, defend why and how not forgiving that person will benefit you.

_____
_____
_____
_____
_____
_____
_____
_____
_____
_____
_____
_____
_____
_____
_____
_____
_____
_____
_____
_____

EIGHT

COURT DAY

It's finally here. Court day. I pray that in the previous chapters you have done the worksheets and that revelations have occurred in your life. If you thought you needed to evict these nasty tenants from your life before, I pray that you are 100% certain now. I also pray that you know and have thought about how your life could be different if you take advantage of the complete authority given to you.

Don't be nervous about this court date. The awareness you now have is all you need to prove your case. Get ready for a victory!

Raise your hand if you love court shows like Judge Mathis, Judge Judy and Divorce Court. If you don't love these shows then I'm sure you have seen them or one like them. If not, it goes a little something like this. People who are suing someone in real life handle their cases on a nationally televised platform instead of their local courthouse. Typically, these are small claims cases so there is a limit in terms of monetary damages they can ask for.

The cases involve scenarios such as being bitten by a neighbor's dog, your friend having an accident in your car or someone failing to pay money they agreed to pay for a service.

There aren't any lawyers involved, each participant has to represent themselves. They are allowed to gather and present as much evidence and witnesses they think they need to accurately represent their version of the events.

I like these shows not for the plaintiffs, but for the judges. I love the street/urban appeal that Judge Mathis has to offer. He isn't a fluffy, silver spoon fed judge. Rather, he is from the streets of Detroit, a person with a past who wants to help others and has a real connection with his fans.

I like the no-nonsense approach of Judge Judy. She really doesn't have time for games, she bases all of her judgements on logic and her words may sting but she is rarely wrong in what she says. I like the almost therapeutic approach of Judge Lynn Toler on Divorce Court. She knows that people don't get married to get divorced and tries to get the litigants to decide if divorce is really what they want.

Each of these judges have a different approach to handling cases and it works for each of them very well. If people are on one of these shows it's because they choose to be. Cases aren't selected randomly. If I had to guess, I would say it's because the plaintiff thinks that based on the cases they have seen in front this judge before, they have a chance at winning.

In your case, the judge that you will present your case to is the one true God. No, this isn't JUDGEMENT where you have to give an account of your life's work, but you going before God and presenting your case (your life) to him and asking His help in evicting the unpleasant tenants, so that you may live peacefully under His promises.

God is for you! Do not be afraid to go before Him and present your case. He is waiting to rule in your favor. "What do you think? With God on our side like this, how can we lose? If God didn't hesitate to put everything on the line for us, embracing our condition and exposing himself to the worst by sending his own Son, is there anything else he wouldn't gladly and freely do for us? And who would dare tangle with God by messing with one of God's chosen? Who would dare even point a finger? The one who died for us-who was raised to life for us- is in the very presence of God at this very moment sticking up for us.

Do you think anyone is going to be able to draw a wedge between us and Christ's love for us? There is no way! Not trouble, not hard times, not hatred, not hunger, not homelessness, not bullying threats, not backstabbing, not even the worst sins listed in Scripture. They kill us in cold blood because they hate us. We're sitting ducks and they pick us off one by one.

None of this fazes us because Jesus loves us. I'm absolutely convinced that nothing, nothing living or dead, angelic or demonic, today or tomorrow, high or low, thinkable or unthinkable, absolutely nothing can get between us and God's love because of the way that Jesus our Master has embraced us." Romans 8:31-37 (MSG)

Although presenting your case to God will be a lot like legal court, there are some differences. First, this case won't be aired on TV or seen on the docket at your local courthouse. This case will be handled in prayer with only you and God present.

You don't have to worry about saying the right thing, you only have to be desperately and brutally honest. When you are talking to God and asking for His help to save your life, you can't afford not to be.

Secondly, do not dress to impress. When we think about court and the people in court, how are they all dressed? Men and women alike are in nice suits, some even tailored to their bodies. There are fancy briefcases and embroidered shirts, maybe even a pair of red bottomed shoes or two. Hair is fried, dyed and laid to the side and faces are beat for the Gods. People are stiff, sitting up straight and not speaking unless spoken to. God doesn't want to see that. He doesn't want to see the image you portray to the world when you come to Him pleading for your life. God wants to see the real you, the broken, beat down, discouraged, afraid, hurt and damaged you.

When you go to present your case to God in prayer, it should be in a place of what is often called "naked prayer". When you are praying a "naked prayer" it doesn't mean that you are actually naked, but that you are not covering up anything. Christians often get in the habit of praying out of habit. That's when you pray just because or in front of other people to impress them and sometimes to try to impress God.   When you are praying a naked prayer, you don't care about any of that. It means that you don't care who may hear, you don't care who is around and you really need God to hear you.

Let's take a look at Nehemiah 1:4. Nehemiah was an esteemed aide to the king. As a matter of fact, he was a cupbearer. In biblical times a popular way to kill people was with poison. To avoid such a tragic death, kings employed men they trusted with their lives to sample their foods and drinks before they did to be sure that it wasn't poisoned.

This wasn't a job given to just anybody so to have earned the trust and respect of the king, Nehemiah had to be of good character. Nehemiah was a descendant from Jerusalem but had never been there. He asked around to see what had been going there and learned that Jerusalem was basically in ruin. He learned that his people were in distress and that the wall that once protected the city had been burned down. This was important because in biblical days people built walls around cities and towns to protect them from outsiders and invasions. To learn that his hometown was defenseless and his people are suffering was heartbreaking to Nehemiah. In 1:4 he said

"So it was, when I heard these words that I sat down and wept and mourned for many days. I was fasting and praying before the God of heaven."

Notice, he didn't say he went home and did this. Right then and there, he wept and prayed to God. He didn't care what anybody thought of him, but he wanted God to know that he was hurting and needed his help to make a change. He was bold enough to ask God exactly for what he needed to go see about his people. The text proves that he thought long and hard about what it was in detail, but he knew he needed mercy from the king to begin with.

As the months, yes months went on, the king noticed that Nehemiah was not himself. This was of utmost importance to the king because if Nehemiah was sick, then the king could be on his way to sickness as well. Boldly, but respectfully, Nehemiah let it be known that he needed to go to Jerusalem. To his surprise, the king's answer was "Well, when will you be back?" Not only did the king give permission for him to go, but because Nehemiah had thought about what he needed, he asked the king for a list of other things to get him on his journey.

During my first naked prayer, I could only cry. I had learned that the Holy Spirit could interpret our moans and groans so I decided to let it do what it was intended to do. I was tired of thinking. I was tired of believing that I wasn't good enough. I was over letting those thoughts win. I had in fact started to become the confident me again. I had won the battle over shame already, so I thought. I told God that I was making decisions for Him from there on out. I knew that He had what was best for already planned out with my name on it and I was tired of talking myself out of it. I don't know how long I was down there or if anyone heard. I didn't care. I got up a changed woman.

Naked prayer is the sum of the "Grounds for Eviction" questions. As you would for any court case, review your exhibits before you go in to see the judge. God already knows the exhibits of course so this review isn't for Him. It's for you.

It's to remind you of the things you have pushed back into your mind and have forgotten about. It's to remind you of the decisions you felt forced to make out of Guilt and Shame. It's to remind you of how successful you have been in this life thing on your own. That was sarcasm. You haven't been nearly as successful as you will be once Guilt and Shame are gone from your property.

In doing this naked prayer, you want to be sure to practice repentance (confess your sins) and accepting the responsibility you hold for making the choices you did. Throughout the book, I was careful to use phrases like "Guilt and Shame influenced me" and "Guilt and Shame led me to believe" because I don't want anyone to shift blame.

I made several bad choices out of guilt and shame and that was simply because I was too proud to ask God for help. I thought I was big and bad enough to handle my problems on my own and I was not. I am still not strong enough to handle my problems on my own today and that's just fine with me because I know now that I serve a God who is. I lost friends, jobs and opportunities, time with my son and family as a result of living in Guilt and Shame. Those were simply the consequences I had to pay, but it was not the end of the line for me and neither shall it be for you.

Thirdly, these are no small claims but there will be no lawyers involved. This isn't like regular court where it's best you don't represent yourself. You are the best representation in this courtroom. No one can tell the horrors, tragedies, sleepless nights or self-defeating habits you have encountered as a result of guilt and shame. Only you can testify how these tenants have are ruining your life. Only you can testify to how badly you want change. Be open and honest confessing to God your many sins. Be open and honest and willing to accept His plan for your life.

Maybe you can't think of all the things you've done or all of the people you hurt. Maybe you can't explain how terribly you this eviction. If you fit into one of these categories then do what I did and simply cry out to God.

"In the same way, the Spirit helps us in our weakness. We do not know what we ought to pray for, but the Spirit himself intercedes for us through wordless groans. And he who searches our heart knows the mind of the Spirit, because the Spirt intercedes for God's people in accordance with the will of God." Romans 8:26-27

Do you think that it is a surprise to God that sometimes life beats you up so bad that you can't even think straight? It's not! God is a God that loves you so much, that He has already prepared and sent a helper to be readily available to you. God has sent us a gift. That is the Holy Spirit, the most important tool for this court day and it is here for you to use!

Don't be confused and think that I am referring to speaking in tongues at this point. Though the Holy Spirit does interpret those as well, in this case Paul is referring to those times such as you may be having right now where you simply don't know what to pray for. These stories and words have opened up and hopefully helped you to heal old wounds, you aren't sure of how to be this new person but you know that a new person is what you want to be. This is when you cry out to God and trust that He will understand.

With that, you are ready to present your case. Yes, in 3 easy steps. Be in private, be naked in prayer and be your own spokesperson. Presenting your case ought to feel better than walking into class to take an open book test that you've actually studied for.

Presenting your case ought to feel better than walking into an interview and the hiring manager has already told you they want to give you the job based on your resume and you have to do the interview for formality. Presenting your case ought to feel better than going to the ATM at 12:03 to withdraw money deposited at 12:00. In all these cases there is something that can go wrong, just because this is life, but chances are you have this in the bag!

The same goes for this case. There is no Judge Judy, Judge Mathis or any other person on this earth to convince in this matter. The Judge over your case is your Heavenly Father. The Judge over this case is your creator who made you to be strong, victorious and free.

There is no condemnation here. Humbling yourself and admitting that you need help will not only get the eviction notice signed, but help along the way. Believe it or not, your strength will be found in your weakness. That mean admitting that you are weak, to God, will cause Him to make you stronger.

"Humble yourselves before the Lord and He will lift you up." James 4:10 (NIV)

"So do not fear, for I am with you; do not be dismayed, for I am your God. I will strengthen you and help you; I will uphold you with my righteous hand." Isaiah 41:10 (NIV)

I can't say this enough.

God is for you.

He wants you to win.

You will win with Him.

God is for you. He wants you to win.

You will with Him. God is for you.

He wants you to win.

You will with Him.

LET'S PRAY

Dear God,

Thank you for preparing me for this court day. I am ready to get a clean slate but I know that starts with getting "naked" in prayer. Understand and work on the unspoken issues of my heart. Cleanse me like never before and let this court day be a close and personal encounter with you.

Amen

GROUNDS FOR EVICTION

Do you have any doubts or fears about changing your life?

_____

_____

_____

_____

_____

How do you feel about the prospect of therapy? Is that a service you think you need? Why or why not?

_____

_____

_____

_____

_____

PREPARING YOUR CASE

Review the answers to the questions you have already given to get ready for your naked prayer. Make a list of issues you want to take before God.

RE-ENFORCEMENTS: AFFIRMATIONS

Today is the first day of the best days of my life.

I am whole.

I can do whatever I need to do because God is my strength.

RECESS: COURT DAY

How do you feel after your time in naked prayer? What burdens have been lifted? How will you preserve your current state of mind?

_____

_____

_____

_____

_____

_____

_____

_____

_____

_____

_____

_____

_____

_____

_____

_____

_____

_____

NINE

THE EVICTION

Based on the evidence presented a decision has been reached. In the case of You versus Guilt and Shame, God finds in favor of you! Guilt and Shame have been found guilty of wreaking havoc in your life. Effective immediately Guilt, Shame and any tenants they have illegally subleased to are evicted from your property!

It is ok to celebrate right now. Go ahead! Sing your praises to God! Shout Hallelujah! Say thank you God! Stomp your feet, clap your hands, cry, dance, do whatever you have to do to let God know that you have felt His deliverance. If you don't "feel" different, that is ok. Praise anyway because it is done. I'll wait.

Praise Break

Whew! Boy, I tell you, there's nothing like a praise break. There is no better feeling than praising The Lord for what He has done OR what He is about to do in your life. As a maturing Christian, I still have moments where doubt tries to creep in and for a second, a tiny little second, and I may wonder how I am going to get out of whatever pickle I have gotten myself into. Just when I remember that I am not all powerful but serve a God who is, He shows up and eats that whole pickle! There is no one who can stop that praise.

Those mid pickle praises are the most exciting to me. It's like seeing a gift under a Christmas tree with your name on it on December 13. You know there is something for you but sadly you have to wait on it. Praising God before my breakthrough gives me that same excitement because I have no idea what

He is going to do. I know that whatever I need is right there, wrapped pretty with a bow and name tag that says "Erica" and nobody can take it away from me. Unless, like when I was growing up, I started to lose my mind around Christmas. The snow days, the candy, oh and that mixed popcorn would have me all wound up and next thing I know my mother would turn into the one who bought Christmas and took it back.

For those of you who are not "feeling" different, don't be like 8 year old me and get your Christmas taken away! I beg of you to know and trust that God has your breakthrough all ready for you. My mom would always break down and let me have Christmas, after all she only wants to see me happy. Feeling like I wasn't going to have anything on Christmas morning made those 2 weeks seem like 2 years.

It made the promised day seem so much further away. That's how the enemy is dealing with you. Whatever God has for you, is for you and no man, no power, no principality can take that from you. However, if you give up the good fight, if you don't press on, if you don't go for it will only prolong the time between now and living the life God intended for you to have.

Whether you feel like the world has been lifted off your shoulders or you just aren't quite sure, mark this day on your calendar, remember it and celebrate it every year. This is the one piece of this book that I haven't lived myself. I noted earlier, the day I had my first naked prayer, but I don't remember what date it was. I remember my start date at the job I got so I know it was around March but I think that having that day forever branded as a day to celebrate and look forward to would be a good tool to have. This is a day worth remembering, a day worth celebrating. This is the day that you have changed your life!

Your next step would be to email me letting me know that you have had your day in court. I will send you a bottle of Holy oil, rub that in your temple twice a day for 7 days and you will never hear Guilt, Shame or any of their associates ever again, for the rest of your life. Does that seem too good to be true? That's because it is! That's not how this works. Sorry if you got your hopes up! As you've probably heard time and time again, realizing that there is a problem and deciding to do something about it is the first step. Evicting Guilt and Shame is just the beginning! Did you really think that the enemy would let go of your mind so easily? No way Jose!

Now that Guilt and Shame have been notified that their time is coming to an end, you have to set ground rules for your property and enforce them. Enforcing the rules of this eviction will have to be a deliberate, every day (and sometimes ALL day) process.

When you wake up to face the day, you have to do it with a goal in mind. That goal should simply be to do your best, give it your best and live THAT DAY guilt and shame free. Don't think of this as a feeling that you have to stretch the rest of your life. Whether you are an 18 year old high school graduate or a 65 year old retiree, the rest of your life is a long time. It's best to take things day by day.

You have to deliberately make up your mind to change your mind. What you think matters and actually determines your life. Before you have a feeling or an attitude about any and every thing, it starts out as a thought. It's often assumed that you have feelings first then thoughts on that feeling. It's actually the other way around.

A thought is first formed in your mind, either on your own accord or a seed planted by The Holy Spirit or the enemy. You then process that thought and the outcome determines the feelings which then develop into your attitude. Say you go to work and on the way in, you think "Oh, this is going to be a bad day, I can just feel it." Already you are preparing yourself for a bad day.

The thought processes and maybe you begin to think of the last time you had a bad day at work or try to predict exactly how the shift will go badly. In a matter of seconds, because our brains work very fast, you have processed that thought into a feeling and attitude of negativity.

What I'm saying is that what you think determines everything else about you're your thoughts determine whether or not you'll shower, pray, comb your hair, treat others nicely, give that homeless man a dollar or even love yourself. As people we tend to get caught up in thinking that "I can't help what I think." and the truth is we can. Changing your thoughts, changing your mindset is something that is hard but possible with God.

By recognizing that are thoughts are OURS and controllable, we have to actively use our mind. We can't go through life letting things happen and following the thoughts of this world. It's a fact that we will have thoughts that are not of God and sometimes we will fall victim to those thoughts. We can train ourselves to take notice of our thoughts and control the way we want them to go. Guilt and Shame are just thoughts, it's when we process those thoughts as though we can't control them that they manifest into negative feelings and attitudes. The answer to this problem is to be a deliberate, active thinker.

Have you ever heard the saying "An idle mind is the devil's playground." I can remember very clearly hearing it for the first time in 5th grade from one of my teachers. One day, as she came in late and, I had finished an assignment given by the on-staff teacher's aide just as she walked in. She thanked and dismissed the aide, said good morning and asked how far along we were on the assignment. I told her I had just finished and she told me to read ahead in the book. I groaned what I thought was under my breath "

Why do I always have to get extra work? This isn't fair!"

She heard me, as most teachers have the power of super hearing, and asked me to repeat myself loud and clear.

Of course I cleaned it up and said "I finished my work and I think that I shouldn't have to do extra."

She asked me "So what do you want to do instead?"

I said "I don't know."

She explained "I give you extra work to keep you from getting in trouble. When you finish early you think that means you can talk with your neighbor or pretend to you have to use the restroom and roam the halls because you aren't using your mind. Keeping you busy is my favor to you because an idle mind is the devil's playground."

I was confused. I asked "What does that mean?"

Her response was "Think about it and keep on living. You'll find out."

I started my work but I was daydreaming about devils running on a playground, sliding down the slide, swinging, playing kickball and other things that I enjoyed. I didn't understand how giving an extra assignment and devils playing freeze tag connected, but I knew better than question her. I went home that day and looked up the definition of idle.

When I got to school early the next day she asked if I had thought about what she said the day before. I told her not really but that I had looked up the definition of idle. She told me to use it in a sentence.

I told her "My pencil is idle when I am reading a book."

"Very good. Now, what do you do on a playground?"

"Play with your friends, have fun." I answered.

"So if you know what idle means and you know what happens on a playground, what do you think "An idle mind is the devil's playground" means.

"It means, if you aren't using your mind, then devil will have fun there." I said.

"Exactly", she said "Do you think the devil's fun will be good for or bad for you?" she asked.

"Bad." I said.

"Right, so that's why we have to keep our minds busy. Do you get it now?" she asked me.

"Yes ma'am"

This was enough to satisfy the curiosity of my 5th grade mind and keep me on track behaviorally for that week. As an adult, I know just how dangerous an idle mind is. The phrase keeps this question in my mind.

If I am not deliberately using my mind, then what?

The answer is simple. The enemy and all of his subordinates have somewhere to play. They have a grand ole time watching us squirm and make mistakes under the false pressure they apply. Making us feel guilty or ashamed most often leads to sin remember? Even though Jesus died on the cross for our sins in turn granting us forgiveness for ALL sins, most people feel bad when they sin. When we sin, it makes us feel far away from God. Most times sin leads to more sin which leads to trouble and deep, dark places. That is when we think "There can't be a God in heaven if I've ended up in this situation." Thoughts like these lead to a sin filled life or at least a life filled with unbelief and either way that's a win for the enemy. In order to avoid going back to these places, we have to think on purpose.

Have you ever seen the results of someone being evicted? If you have, that situation has gone too far. Just as we had to gather evidence and present the case before a judge, landlords and property owners have to do the same thing. They don't have legal right to go around putting people's things on the curb. There has been eviction proceeding paperwork filed, the property owner and tenants were both notified of a court date, a hearing was had and favor was granted in one direction or another and an exit date was given.

The tenants, most times, don't have to vacate the premises immediately, though they can. The judge normally grants them 30 days to gather all of their things and find another place to live. When the tenant doesn't move on those orders and stays in the property, that is when the court is notified again and the sheriff's office is given permission to let's say "help them out". At this point the tenant is breaking the law by not following judge's order. The property owner has to do whatever it takes to get them out.

You have already decided to evict Guilt and Shame, God has judged in your favor and it is up to you to stand on that judgement. You are the property owner here. Are you going to wait 30 days to begin to live clearly and free as God intended? Are you going to wait and see if they leave on their own? Thinking about the fun these devils have had on your playground, do you think they are going to leave on their own accord? Of course not! The good thing is we do not have to abide by the laws set in your state in the matter of this eviction. Instead of waiting 30 days you can begin to force them out now!

Guilt and Shame aren't people that we can pick them up and set them outside. They are thoughts in our mind and the force we will use to get them out are thoughts as well. We won't be using regular, puny thoughts but big thoughts that look a little like Sheriff's Deputies. They are big and strong, they have meaning and a job to do. They wear their shiny badges proud on their chest and they mean business.

Try as they might, Guilt and Shame have no hope against them. In fact, these thoughts are so powerful, let's call them affirmations. An affirmation is a thought or mantra that you say over and over until it manifests itself in your life. We will use affirmations to rebuke the critical demons at work in your life to make room for the tenants God intended us to have.

What you say to yourself, or "self-talk" is more important than what anybody else in the world can ever say to you. If I tell you that you are the most beautiful girl in the world but you constantly tell yourself otherwise, your own thoughts will take precedence. You can use whatever you choose to affirm guilt and shame's exit from your property. In choosing your affirmations, you want to choose something that builds you up as well.

For example, while "I will not live in guilt." Is a good choice "I will not make decisions out of guilt. I will do what is best for me and the situation while being fair to myself and others." Is a better one because it gives you an attitude to work towards and something to hope for. If you think that creating an affirmation is a daunting task, I agree. While I was knee deep in my eviction process and deciding that I was going to think and live on purpose, I chose to use scripture as affirmation. What better than the word of God to change your life?

95

That's a rhetorical question obviously.

One of the first ones I chose as an affirmation was "Seek the Lord with all your heart and lean not on your own understanding." Proverbs 3:5 (NIV)

How smart are you? How smart are you in comparison to God? How strong are you? How strong are you in comparison to God? How much do you know about the world? How much do you know about the world in comparison to God? No matter what we think we know, we have no idea.

We, as humans, cannot be trusted. We are prone to hurt, harm and danger as well as the attacks of the enemy. Those of us who are fighting guilt and shame are especially untrustworthy because we weren't thinking clearly. The enemy has a way of making us overthink about what we need and want when all the while God knows what it is best. Even in situations where things are not optimal, God can still use them for your good and His glory.

Take me being molested for example. There is nothing good about being molested as a child, not a single solitary thing and I will promise you that. What God did with that situation was teach me about perseverance, trusting Him and even forgiveness and compassion. During my addiction to pleasing people, I became so dependent on their opinions it broke me down. God delivered me from that so that I can learn to lean only on him.

There is no telling why you have experienced what you have or what is in your future. It's not for us to beat ourselves up over what happened or to try to predict what will happen. What we can do is desire to spend time with God, to read and study His word, to perfect a relationship with Him which will lead to us trusting Him.

It is human nature for us to survive and try to figure things out but in comparison to God, we are like children who need our Father to show us the way.

One of the biggest sub-leasers to Guilt and Shame in my house was Fear. Fear absolutely controlled me. Hands down. However, once I was done with Guilt and Shame, Fear had to go as well. It's like when your little brother's friends come over and your little brother leaves the room but his friend is still sitting there. You're thinking "What are you still doing here?"

Every so often Fear would come flouncing around trying to get back in but I had made my mind up that it would not. What enforced it for me was 2 Timothy 1:7. "For God hath not given us the spirit of fear; but of power, and of love, and of a sound mind (self-discipline, self-control)"

Whenever I became afraid of being honest about a mistake I made or speaking up for myself, I would think about this verse. That's how it started out, as just a thought. This made me think things like "If God didn't GIVE me fear, then where is it coming from?"

I wanted each and everything I thought and did to be a reflection of God and being fearfully evidently wasn't that. Eventually, I began to murmur the thought and finally could say it out loud to fear in any situation and even in front of people. I couldn't have cared less that in the middle of a conversation I recited a bible verse. I began to feel powerful, I began to feel in control, I began to feel as though I could love myself and others because every day (sometimes several times a day) I reminded myself that this is how God created me to be.

When Guilt and Shame knocked on the door to tell me that I could never change, I screamed this verse at them from the comfort of my guilt and shame free home. "Do not conform to the pattern of this world, but be transformed by the renewing of your mind. Then you will be able to test and approve what God's will is—his good, pleasing and perfect will." Romans 12:2 (NIV)

Don't fit in to what everybody else does or simply what feels comfortable to you. Be changed, by the renewing of your mind. This means that your mind can be made fresh and strong. Living with guilt and shame ridden lives is a worldly thing to do because it is from the dark spirits of this world.

This scripture told me that I could be changed, I could be free, if I only changed or renewed my mind! With a new mind, I could see and test God's will, and His will is perfection! Because I told myself this every day (and sometimes several times a day) I began to think differently and know that my life could be on the track to perfection, which is fulfilling God's will. I knew that I wouldn't be perfect and wouldn't beat myself up WHEN I made mistakes, but I knew that going wholeheartedly after the will of God through a changed mind would give me peace like never before.

A strong mind was already given to us but since an idle mind is the devil's playground, the ways of the world weaken us and we get lost and sidetracked. When we renew, THEN, we will be able to means observe, examine, evaluate and discern what God's will is for us.

Sometimes a sub-leaser named Doubt would drop by. He would come and say things like "Girl, are you crazy? We've been here all your life! You can't just up and change like that! You aren't strong enough. We are a part of you now. Let us back in and we will forget this whole eviction thing ever happened." Want to know what I said to him?

2 Corinthians 10:5 (NLV) says "We break down every thought and proud thing that puts itself up against the wisdom of God. We take hold of every thought and make it obey Christ."

When my thoughts would make their way back to my default setting, I used this affirmation to remind me that Guilt and Shame had no power. This let me know that by asking a few questions I could break down their arguments like they were guilty defendants on a nightstand and I was an award winning prosecutor. I hold the power to making them obey Christ and if He says they have no right in my mind then they had to go.

I actually would talk to myself and figure out if I was experienced deserved or undeserved guilt and shame. This was extremely present in work situations. I had one of those "almost but not quite" supervisors during my eviction process. She was one of those supervisors where everything was almost acceptable, it almost fits the criteria but 9 times out 10 she would find something wrong with the work that was turned in. This wasn't with just me but with all employees. There were times I would work on a project all night and then wake up early to proofread and double check only to hear that what I presented was with fault. Some may say that being able to find area for improvement is the mark of a good leader and that may be true. In my case being constantly told that my work wasn't pleasing to my supervisor was a source of stress and added to my depression.

I was addicted to the approval of others which was set on by guilt. When guilt would try to tell me that I was once again a failure, I would talk back.
"Was the work understandable?"
"Did I make good use of the time I was allowed?"
"Was the work turned in on time?"
"Did I do the best I could with the instructions I had?"

If the answers to these questions were "yes" then I had nothing to feel bad about. Like the old saying goes "You can't win them all" and trust me, in this job I barely won at all. I stopped taking it personally as though the supervisor's dissatisfaction with the project was a personal reflection on me. I would try again if given the opportunity to or simply move on to the next task, taking the notes provided. Being in this situation had become familiar and I was always fearful. Fearful to stand up for my work, fearful of being sent home for the day or week and fearful of losing my job. In these times, I would also tell myself "God did not give me a spirit of fear, but of power, love and self-control." Saying THIS would give me the power to break down those negative thoughts and ultimately leave the office feeling like a winner.

There was one scripture in particular that I said every day (and sometimes several times a day) because in my mind, it reigned supreme. This was the scripture that revved my engine and got me started. "I can do all things through Christ who strengthens me!" Phillippians 4:13

I love this verse because it doesn't say "Everybody, but Erica can do all things because they are better than her." It doesn't say "Erica can do somethings because she is good at them and other things she just won't be able to do." It doesn't say "Erica can do somethings if she cheats her way." It says "I, Erica, can do ALL things through Christ who strengthens me." Now you read that verse out loud. Do you know what that means? It means YOU can do all things through Christ who strengthens you!

"I can do all things" is important and empowering on its own accord. The latter of the scripture is like getting under a warm blanket in a soft bed. "I can do all things" feels so good, just like laying down in a bed at a 4 star hotel. I'm sure 5 is better but hey, I can only speak for up to 4 stars. If you tell enough people about how awesome this book is, maybe, just maybe I can sleep in a 5 star bed. But I digress. So laying in that soft bed, in that comfort that you can do all things is good right. What's better than that? When you pull those covers up to your chin and the blanket is thick and will keep you warm, but it's not heavy! Oh, that's the best. That's what "through Christ who strengthens me" feels like to me. It lets me know that I'm not alone. It lets me know that I don't have to do this on my own. It lets me know that the Savior of the world, not just me, THE WORLD, not just St. Louis, MO, THE WORLD has my back and will be my strength.

I started out with these scriptures and eventually worked my way to ten. If you want to start out with one, two or ten, it's completely up to you. I would pick a certain time every day to repeat the scripture to myself over and over as a form of mind training or meditation. People often get scared of the word "meditation" because they think it's a form of communicating with spirits and a host of other beliefs. Meditation simply means "to spend time in quiet contemplation". It's just a matter of sitting somewhere alone, in quiet and thinking about something deliberately. In fact, meditation is a godly action as proved in Joshua 1:8: "Keep this Book of the Law always on your lips; meditate on it day and night, so that you may be careful to do everything written in it. Then you will be prosperous and successful."

If we make our affirmations words of scripture and meditate on them, we will live our lives doing what is instructed. If we constantly think about the word of God and the promises He made to us, then our actions, attitudes and feelings will be representative of that. If we have affirmations walking around our property, then guilt and shame will have to flee. Affirmations will have to be the first tool of defense in enforcing the favor God granted you. They will walk around and patrol the place, planting seeds of the fruit of the spirit all throughout. You can pray to God and ask Him to lead you to scripture affirmations, you can look online or even ask around. I also have listed some in the appendix and have broken down into categories.

While I believe that having the affirmations around will lead you away from guilt and shame, I believe that there are two more tools to use that go hand in hand. Counseling and support. Although we have won the case of eviction and have some affirmations around keeping things in order, it's important to get some outside perspective, if only for a little bit. Some of you probably need counseling, some of you don't, but you all need outside support. Changing our minds, therefore our lives, will be a hard thing and nothing beats having a friend to help you through that.

I could lie to you all and make it seem like this is the end of the line and it's not. Even with my affirmations and renewed mind, there were, and will be days when I just need that push from a friend or family member to get me through. The enemy has been winning as long as you thought that living with Guilt and Shame was normal. You didn't know that there was any other way to live. Now that you know and are making strides in changing that, his attacks will only get stronger. Don't let that deter you, remember, in Christ you have already won. The victory is already yours.

Take the first chapter of 1 Kings for example. In it, King David is sick and appears that he will be dying soon. Previously he has already promised that Solomon would be the new king. Adonijah, who was handsome and strong, declared himself king. He sacrificed cattle, had chariots drawn up and even gathered supporters in this cause. Solomon didn't have to go and ruin the party, stomp in there murdering people or causing a scene. Solomon didn't have to go begging God or David. A promise was made to and for him all he had to do was allow God to see it through. God worked though other people who made it known to King David what was going on and he made sure that Solomon was crowned properly. Everything happened the way it was supposed to. Adonijah found out what was going on and ended up proclaiming that he was scared of Solomon and asking him to spare his life.

Whatever is for you, is yours. There is nothing nobody can do to take that away from you. As a matter of fact, He will send you help and support to make sure things go in your favor.

Before I started my eviction process I was in a depression so deep I couldn't even see it. I went to work, took care of my son and even managed to have good times with my friends on the weekend. My supervisor at work noticed though, and pretty much laid out to me that my job depended on me going to therapy to see what my depression was about. I didn't think I was depressed at all but I went because, what else was I going to do?

I knew that I didn't want someone looking at me and telling me all the things they learned from a college course book. I also didn't want someone to give me a pill to suppress anything I was dealing with, if I was dealing with anything at all. I read a book on different types of therapy and figured that cognitive therapy was what I wanted.

I wanted, if need be, to figure out a way to "fix" myself. I was finally starting to take this God thing seriously and wanted to see what He said about depression. I wanted a Christian counselor. I wanted someone who could help me in according to what the Word of God said.

After sitting on the couch and nonchalantly telling her my story she told me about myself in a way that I had never heard before. She told me that I was blank, that even in telling her about being molested I conveyed no emotion. She told me that legally my supervisor could not force me into therapy and asked what was it that led me there? She told me that she saw signs of PTSD and depression all over me. At the end, she told me that God loves me and that the three of us could get things all straightened out.

I was shocked because I went to basically vent about things in my life. I went so that I could have a safe and secure soundboard for saying all of the things I had been afraid to say and not have to worry about it getting back to me. I went to keep my job. I didn't go to therapy to be told that I was depressed and that I had PTSD. That's the bonus of getting help with this eviction. Being our own judge, we never see ourselves clearly. We always see ourselves as the Super men and women we think we are. Most of you probably didn't pick this book up yourselves, instead it was given or suggested for you.

Had I not went to see her or someone, I wouldn't have had an eviction. I would still be somewhere beaten down and depressed while portraying an air of false confidence. Worse off, I probably would have found the strength to go through with suicide. Having someone outside of myself assist in building me up was exactly what I needed.

If you are thinking a thought that is telling you that counseling is not for you, let me try to convince you.

"I can't afford therapy."

Some therapists offered income based services. You can try searching for "income based Christian counseling" and I'm sure something in your area will populate.

Most people who get into therapy/counseling field don't do it for the money, but because they have a deep desire to help others therefor are a little flexible with their pricing.

"I don't have time for therapy."

I didn't either. Most therapists only work business hours. Some may offer phone, Skype or even FaceTime sessions. Some therapists offer Saturday or evening hours. Whatever your need is, there is someone for you.

"I don't really need therapy. I'm ok"

Didn't I tell you I didn't need therapy either and this lady told me I had PTSD and was mildly depressed? While we are dealing with surface issues, there may be something deeper waiting to be uncovered.

"I don't want to tell anybody my problems. I think I'll be better off just keeping it between me and God."

This thought is the epitome of what your unintended tenants want you to think. Whether you are ashamed of your past or fearful of being judged, these are not valid reasons to avoid seeking counsel in getting past this. God wants you to confide and trust in Him, but frankly speaking, we need each other just as much. God gave us the ability to create life so that we can love each other. Part of that includes being able to give life to another when he/she is down. How will anyone know that you need help if you are hiding behind a mask of perfection? Trust me when I say, if you are hiding, you probably aren't doing as good of a job as you think!

James 5:16 says, "Therefore, confess your sins to one another and pray for one another, that you may be healed. The prayer of a righteous person has great power as it is working."

When you let someone in, you have to be sure that it is someone you trust. If you are thinking about confiding in the person who you gossip with, they aren't the one. The point of sharing burdens and confessing sins to one another is not for your business to travel the world. The point is to have a person agreeing with you in prayer. You want to pick someone who is trustworthy, who Honors God and wants to see you win.

LET'S PRAY

Father God,

Thank you for judging in my favor! Help the eviction take root. Help me identify the help you"ll be sending me. Give me peace in knowing this life has already been created for me and is waiting for me to walk into it.

Amen

KEEPING IT CLEAN

In your own words, how will changing your mindset help you keep guilt and shame out of your life?

_____

_____

_____

_____

_____

_____

Write a list of qualities that will make a person trustworthy. Do you know someone like that? If so, pray and ask God if they would be a good support partner in this eviction. If not, ask God to help you.

_____

_____

_____

_____

_____

_____

RE-ENFORCEMENTS: AFFIRMATIONS

I am free from the guilt and shame of my past.

I am free to live the life God has planned for me.

God will make His plans known to me and provide a way for me to fulfill them.

RECESS: THE EVICTION

How did your previous mindset/way of thinking invite guilt and shame to stay in your life? How will your new mindset change your life? What do you see your life becoming as a result of your new thought process?

_____

_____

_____

_____

_____

_____

_____

_____

_____

_____

_____

_____

_____

_____

_____

TEN

LEAVE IT ON THE CURB

This will by far be my favorite part of the book to write. Before we get into why, let's recap. We started off recognizing that we are children of a God who loves us enough to have a purpose for us.

We addressed that fact that Guilt and/or Shame live our homes and what that looks like. We realized they rarely travel alone and most times have sub-leased space on property without our knowledge.

We served them with eviction notices letting them know that they had to go and that we are on a road to find out and pursue what our purpose is.

We had our day in court with God who of course ruled in our favor and we brought in re-enforcements (affirmations) to get them out.

That's a lot of ground to have covered and I hope you are proud of yourself because I sure am proud of you.

Do you have a hard time letting things go? This question isn't in reference to people or situations. Are you one of those people who just can't throw away anything?

Do you still have finger paint portraits from kindergarten? What about those shoes you bought to go with that sweater and have never worn either? I can't sympathize with that one because I throw away everything. If I'm not using it and can't see myself using it then it's out the door. This probably results in me having to buy things over but I just can't stand the clutter. I pray that you become more like me in this area for this chapter of the book.

We know that your previous tenants have been evicted and they, in essence, are on the curb outside of your property. They have been discarded! They are trash, to be taken away!

Do not, I repeat, DO NOT BRING IT BACK IN THE HOUSE! LEAVE IT ON THE CURB! I REPEAT, LEAVE IT ON THE CURB!

Going back to that junk is like (and several of us can relate, including myself) losing a bunch of weight and then going back to your old ways. In this area, it's important to take a resolve to not turn back. Will there be times where you do? Only if you allow it.

There is a particular area of sin that I fight almost daily. It's a constant struggle and most times I lose. However, for a period of about 3 weeks I had been winning. I began to tell myself that it was over and was ready to have a party! One day, out of nowhere, the feeling comes over me. Stronger than I have ever felt before. I tried and tried to resist, what felt like my hardest at the time.

Next thing I know, I was knee deep in it. When my sin session was over, Guilt AND Shame knocked on the door almost immediately. "Girl, look at you!" "How could you do such a thing?" "I thought you said you weren't going to do that anymore!" "All that work wasted, so I guess means you're going back to your old ways?" Because the feeling was familiar to me, I began to sink. I could literally feel myself draining.

That's when I remembered that I had already evicted Guilt and Shame. I remembered that they didn't live with me anymore and just so happen to be in the neighborhood, peering into my windows. I imagined looking out the window at them and pulling the curtains shut.

I immediately went to God in prayer at that time. I confessed my sin and asked for His help and forgiveness. I didn't feel instantly better and sometimes you won't either. That's when I began to say my affirmations. "I can do all things through Christ who strengthens me." "I take every thought captive and force it to obey Christ." "I can be renewed by the changing of my mind." After saying these about 3 times each, I did feel better and moved on with my day, guilt free.

Evicting guilt and shame from your house doesn't free you from sin, but it does free you from the bondage of sin. If sin is a box that holds you captive, guilt and shame are the tape that hold the box shut.

Take those Styrofoam packaging nuggets. If we fill a box with them and don't tape it shut, when that box shakes all of the nuggets fall out and are freed. Without Guilt and Shame keeping you trapped, like the Styrofoam nuggets, you can become free with a little shaking.

"Erica, what if I pray, confess my sins and I still don't feel better?"

Sometimes you won't. I can say though, that most times you will. On the occasions that you don't is when you make use of the affirmations. You are trying to change a pattern that has been with you most of your life. Guilt and Shame didn't move in your house quickly, though they are on the outside now, they won't leave quickly.

You will have to shut them down time and time again. This wasn't a quick mess and it won't be a quick fix.

"Ok, I prayed, I said my affirmations, I still feel the same."

This is when you call on God! Remember that you are not in this alone! You won't be able to do this on your own. It's important that you tap into the power and authority afforded to you through The Holy Spirit.

You are no match for the enemy on your own but with the power of the blood you are. You are not fighting to change who you are, God will change you. You are fighting to be available for the change. That's it. You are fighting to have an open mind, free of guilt and shame.

This is also why it's important to have support in this venture. These are the times when you call your prayer warriors, your therapists or whoever it is that God sends to build you up during this time.

"My prayer warrior is 69 and she goes to bed at 6pm. What do I do now?"

I'm glad you asked. THIS is my favorite part.

If you haven't guessed by now, I have a vivid imagination. I want you to think about a NFL player all dressed for the game. He has his pads on his shoulders, his helmet, his special shoes (what are they called, cleats?), his little thigh pads and everything he needs to be protected during the game. Injuries are going to happen, it's a part of the game, but every chance is taken to make the injury have a little impact as possible.

Now ask yourself this, if God can create (because He is the CREATOR) protection for men to throw a ball around a field, wouldn't he create protection for us to live everyday lives? If you said no, read Chapter One again and come back later. For those of you who said yes, you are right! Again, no prize. Here's the thing, the protection is given to you but you can't see it. In order to live this life and fight this fight successfully, you have to wear and believe in the full armor of God.

One day, I sat in a waiting room, I pulled out a travel sized bible and was reading something or another and this guy asked me if I was familiar with Ephesians. I lit up because I was. He asked me to turn to 6:10.

"Finally, be strong in the Lord and his mighty power. Put on the full armor of God, so that you can take your stand against the devil's schemes. For our struggle is not against flesh and blood, but against the rulers, against the authorities, against the powers of this dark world and against the spiritual forces of evil in the heavenly realms.

Therefore put on the full armor of God, so that when the day of evil comes, you may be able to stand your ground and after you have done everything, to stand. Stand firm then, with the belt of truth buckled around your waist, with the breastplate of righteousness in place, and with your feet fitted with the readiness that comes from the gospel of peace in addition to all this, take up the shield of faith, with which you can extinguish all the flaming arrows of the evil one. Take the helmet of salvation and the sword of the spirit which is the word of God."

I highlighted this passage of scripture and eventually God told me what it meant.

BELT OF TRUTH

If you think about it, what does a belt do? It goes around the center point of your body, your waist. Your waist is what is called your center of gravity because that's where your balance is. Your waist being the center of gravity is why you tackle people there during a football game, they will fall. So your belt goes around your waist and does what?

Hold everything together. It's a small strip of leather, in comparison to your body it could even be tiny, but that little thing holds your pants up and keeps your shirt tucked in giving you an appearance of togetherness. A young man could be dressed in $500 jeans, $200 shirt and $800 shoes but if he doesn't have on a simple belt the cost and names associated with the apparel doesn't even matter. He looks sloppy, he is not complete and something is obviously missing. We all need a belt as part of our armor and the figurative belt we have is to be made of the truth.

The truth that we need to have wrapped around our waist, holding us together at all times is that truth of who we are in Christ. The truth is God loves us. He has blessed us with every, not some, but every spiritual blessing in heaven. We are forgiven. We were chosen by God. We are part of God's plan.

BREASTPLATE OF RIGHTEOUSNESS

If you are like me, you are thinking "What in the world is a breastplate?" A breastplate was a metal sheet that went over the front of the Roman soldiers. It went from their shoulders down to their waist. It covered and protected their internal organs. Heart, lungs, stomach and all that other good stuff was protected from swords, flaming arrows and other weapons of the day. In the same way, righteousness is what we should use to protect our internal organs, mainly our heart.

Righteous means to be moral (doing what is right) or virtuous (pure). Righteousness therefore means upholding these things or the act of being these things. If righteousness is to be our breastplate that means doing the right things will protect us. When we do the right thing, there is minimal room for Guilt and Shame to convince us of otherwise. Doing the right thing leaves Guilt and Shame with nothing to hold over your head.

It's like when you have a brother or sister who tells every little thing you do and sometimes you have to give them a little hush money to keep quiet. Guilt and Shame is like that brother or sister and your sanity is the hush money. Except it doesn't work. No amount of your sanity will hush the whispers and sometimes screams of Guilt and Shame. However, doing the right thing leaves them waiting in silence.

SHOES OF PEACE

We know that during these times there were no paved roads or even sidewalks. There were just dirt paths and everybody knew to get out of the way when a horse was coming! You can imagine that when it rained and such that the whole city was full of mud and that people were slipping and sliding everywhere. As a soldier, who has to be ready to fight at all times, could they have had on shoes that allowed them to slip and slide? No. They had special shoes, much like cleats, that allowed them traction when need be. They gave them a little bit of slip resistance so that they could stand to fight. These shoes are what peace is for us.

Our world is going to get slippery. There will be storms. God has not promised us an easy road but to be our strength during the hard times. When life gets rough and the sturdy dirt path turns to mushy mud, let the peace of God be the cleats that leave you able to stand and fight another day. Let the peace of God protect your feet from the rocks, sticks and stones that the enemy will lay out in front of you in efforts to get you back to your old ways. Let the peace of God carry you.

God's peace doesn't have to make sense to us or anybody else. When I was in the midst of chaos, I decided to stop trying to solve every problem and outthink the enemies, spiritual and physical. I decided to be still, be peaceful and let God be God.

One day, the director of the company I worked for, who knew all that was going on in my life said to me "You sure are calm. Everything and everybody else is going crazy."

I told her "That's because I've decided to be at peace no matter what's going on, what anybody else's mood is or how they feel. I can't control any of those things but I can control me, and I've decided that I'll be at peace."

Having the peace of God doesn't mean that you have it all figured out but that you trust Him enough to know that everything will work out for your good.

SHIELD OF FAITH

During wars Roman soldiers had huge shields to protect them. They could use them to block strikes from enemy soldiers during hand to hand combat or to hide under when enemy forces would shoot hundreds of flaming arrows from the sky. The shields were strong and made of impenetrable metal. Though the shields protected the soldiers, they didn't stop the attacks. The attacks were going to happen because that's what goes down during a time of war. The soldiers stay prepared and even when it was regular day in Rome, had the shield wherever they went.

Faith is to be our shield and protection. What is faith? Faith is believing in something that has not happened yet. We have faith that our husbands won't cheat on us. We have faith that our paycheck will be loaded into our bank accounts when they should be. We have faith that our car will start when we turn the key in the ignition.

The one thing that all of these examples have in common is that they can fail. Sometimes husbands cheat, sometimes paychecks aren't there and sometimes cars don't start. The difference in having faith in God is that he can't fail. Whatever He promises will come to be. Don't get that confused with the fact that He may say wait or even no, but He won't fail you. Having faith is believing that no matter the circumstance He will see you through.

Whether we are fighting the enemy close up or he sends an attack from a distance, faith is what we use to cover ourselves. Living daily life is a war. It's a constant battle not to settle into the natural ways of sin that we have and it will be a fight to change your mindset.

There will be attacks and battles, God does not say that there won't be, but if we believe that it will all work for our good and let that cover us, we will make it. Do not go to battle unprotected without your shield. If during a battle a soldier loses his breastplate, his shoes and his belt, if he can hide behind his shield he might just make it to fight another day. We might do the wrong thing, tell a lie or even be disgruntled but when all else fails, if we hold on to our faith, we will survive.

HELMET OF SALVATION

What is a helmet used for? In construction, sports or armed services a helmet has one singular use, to protect your brain. Why is that so important? Your brain is your headquarters! That's where the ship is ran, that is where all the magic happens.

I hope that if you didn't know before reading Eviction Notice, you now know that what you think matters. What you think determines not just your feelings and attitudes but your life. We've learned that our mind is where the enemy begins his attacks. Our sins don't start in our body, but in our mind. We have to first think about it before it is committed. Sin is the open door to Guilt and Shame.

Wearing a helmet of salvation means that knowing that Jesus Christ died for our sins and that we are forgiven is what we use to protect our minds from the enemy. Our salvation is strong, nothing can take it from us.

SWORD OF THE SPIRIT

A sword is sharp on two sides, can be used in many different ways and situations. Used as a weapon a sword can kill or at least put off an enemy for a good while. A sword is an easy weapon to travel with and a light load to bear. A sword, unlike a gun or arrow, doesn't have to be loaded or prepared for use. A sword comes ready to use. A sword does have to be sharpened from time to time. You can keep using it in the same way over and over, but it becomes less effective. I've never used a sword, but I imagine that after every battle soldiers took the time to freshen it up before the next one.

Not knowing when an enemy might attack means always having to stay ready and having a sharp sword is part of that. A dull sword would have to be the worst thing to have in the time of an attack. Protecting yourself from the enemy is one way to preserve life, but I imagine that it would become draining. There is nothing like striking back to give you that push of encouragement to go on. How terrible!

As a soldier of God, the weapon He has given you is His word. Just as sword, the word of God should be your first line of defense in an attack from the enemy. It's sharp, it's direct and there's no second guessing it. There may be many interpretations and that's ok, but the power remains the same. The word of God is full of proof of God's love, promises from God and purpose for your life. The word of God is strong enough to strike down any enemy attack which is why I chose it for myself and recommend it to be your affirmations.

The enemy we are fighting is crafty. If we defeat him in one way, he will try to find another and attack even stronger. The only way to beat him at his mind game is to have the word of God on your mind and on your lips at all times. Keep your sword sharp by studying the word of God always. If you know the truth of the word, Satan won't win against you. The attack may still come, but you are guaranteed a victory. It's the best weapon we have and it's readily available.

There are free bibles at almost every church, free bible apps on every app store and translations that even children can understand. However you have to get the word, then get it. If you can't read, there are Bible CD's and DVD's. If you don't have a DVD/CD player, listen to it online. If you don't have internet access, simply go to a bible based church.

Using these tools ought to be your daily uniform. However, simply telling you that they are available for you to use isn't enough. You have to believe. You have to know it for yourself. You have to trust that just as these tools worked for me, they can work for you too.

As long as He knows that you trust Him, are dependent on Him, are counting on Him, he will show up and show out way more than you can ask or even think! The difference is that if you don't believe, God won't give up on you. He'll keep planting seeds and having people share testimonies when they speak to you or even in books (hint) and He won't leave you. I ask you, knowing that you are in a battle for your mind, your sanity, your life, will you go into battle unprepared or will you take the weapons and protection that believing in God will afford you?

You have made the decision and followed through with evicting Guilt and Shame from your life. They, along with their sub tenants and all of their possessions are on the curb. Unprotected, you aren't strong enough to leave it there. Like a moth to a flame, you will go back. However, suited up as a soldier of God, protected on all fronts by truth, righteousness, peace, faith, salvation and the word of God, you can and will leave it all on the curb.

LET'S PRAY

Father God,

Thank you for weapons and protections for us to use until I see you in heaven. Father, let me be brave and correct in their use. Help me to have your knowledge, wisdom, to seek your face and to be strong, rooted and grounded in you during our coming battles.

Amen

PREPARING FOR BATTLE

Court is over but the battle has just began. The armor of God has been explained, but journal what it means to you in your own words.

_____

_____

_____

_____

_____

If you fail to plan then plan to fail. The best weapon in warfare is preparation. How will you use the full armor of God?

_____

_____

_____

_____

_____

RE-ENFORCEMENTS: AFFIRMATIONS

I have everything I need, to do everything I need.

I am supported by God in all things, in all areas and at all times.

RECESS: KEEPING IT ON THE CURB

After learning about the armor of God, in what ways do you feel prepared for any upcoming battles? How will peace, joy, faith, truth, righteousness and the spirit of God help you in your everyday life?

_____

_____

_____

_____

_____

_____

_____

_____

_____

_____

_____

_____

_____

_____

_____

_____

_____

_____

_____

_____

_____

_____

ELEVEN

MAINTAIN YOUR WHITEBOX

"Free at last, free at last, thank God almighty, we're free at last!"

Dr. Martin Luther King Jr

There are many things that separate us culturally and there are just as many that make us one and the same. Yes, we all have dealt with Guilt and Shame but what about the Saturday morning cleanup? I don't know a person whose mother/father/grandmother/somebody didn't believe that Saturday mornings are made for cleaning

Maybe it wasn't Saturday morning in your house, maybe it wasn't a weekly thing, but we all know when the head of the household is in clean mode there there is no escaping it. In my house it was Saturday mornings. Usually, if my mother was off, she would make us breakfast or we would run errands. When the music of the 60's woke us up on a Saturday morning, we already knew what time it was.

It was time to clean the wall that ran alongside the stairs streaked with dirty hands and juice spills. It was time to pull beds and couches from walls to find lost homework, shoes and Pop Tart wrappers. It was time to do laundry until the only dirty clothes in the house were on our backs. It was time to sweep, mop, vacuum, clean baseboards and organize closets while passing down outgrown clothes.

We hated these mornings primarily because these were the days we had cereal made with real sugar and actual cartoons on Saturday morning. After doing (or half doing) chores all week, the last thing we wanted was to do was a deep clean but it had to be done.

After sweating, feeling like slaves, an argument or 3, the house sparkled. We would light candles and open the windows for some fresh air and after breakfast and baths, enjoy our nice clean and quiet (because we were all worn out from cleaning) house. After the hard work, it paid off.

This feeling of a job well done, is what I pray for you. It's not fun cleaning old junk out of the fridge, but isn't wonderful when you can open the door and no strange smell greets you? I pray that you are relaxing in your new house, quiet and clean with a fresh breeze flowing through.

This has been some a journey for both writer and reader. I have opened up some wounds, learned things about myself and made new resolves in being a better me. While doing these things, I have prayed and prayed that even better things happen for you. I'm so excited for life, I'm excited for change, I'm excited for what God is about to do in our lives. If you are still having a hard time believing, I'm believing in God for you.

I have laid out the tools for you and I pray that you have found them easy to follow, easy to remember and most importantly, easy to use. That's about where the ease ends though. I want you to enjoy the serenity that lives within you now, but know that you are going to have to work to keep your house clean.

"Erica, how do I keep my house clean?"

I'm glad you asked! Now although my actual house is a completely different story, here are 10 Housekeeping Tips to aide you in your fight against Guilt and Shame.

Establish the Head of Household

Throughout this book I have boldly proclaimed the good works of God in my life. I have done that because they are available to work in your life. Most of you are already Christians but with the help of God, I hope this book has found its way into the hands of an unbeliever who is thinking that they just might give this God thing a try. To those of you, I say welcome! In order for this eviction to work, in order to tap into the power of God you have to be born again. You have to acknowledge your sins to God, believe in your heart and confess with your mouth that Jesus is God's son sent to Earth to die for our sins and was raised from the dead 3 days later by the power of God and accept him as your Lord and Savior.

This doesn't have to be a complex prayer, in fact, it is better if it's not. God is a real God and wants you to be real with Him. You can say your own prayer, use the one to follow or start with the one to follow and add on at the end:

Father and God,

I admit that I am a sinner and have sinned against you. I believe that Jesus is your son, sent to Earth to die for the sins of many. I believe that He died so that I may be forgiven. I accept this forgiveness today. I believe that you raised Him from the dead by your own power to be Lord of your people. I accept Him as my Lord and Savior.

Amen

YAY! I'm so excited for those of you who renewed your faith or accepted Christ for the first time. Heaven is rejoicing right now and you should be too!

Now, this is something I'm going to throw in for free, accepting Jesus as your savior is the easy part. You didn't have to do anything but accept it, like a birthday gift. Accepting Him as your Lord, is where your work comes in. If God wanted for Jesus to be our Savior only, He wouldn't have raised Him from the dead. Jesus became our Savior because He died to save us. Once he was dead, that part was complete. He was raised from the dead because He lived a sinless life, therefore worthy to offer us advice and leadership on how to work towards attaining the same. Accepting Him as Lord means to follow His lead. Daily.

Get to Know Him

Even though I have provided you with several examples of the goodness of God, it's nothing like knowing for yourself. Having a relationship with God is a real life "You had to be there!" story. I can give you vivid imagery, cry and shout to convince you but until you know for yourself, a story is all it will ever be.

There are several ways to get to know God, the simplest would be to do your research. Don't go looking in an encyclopedia (do they still make those?) but go to your bible. The Bible is more than "Thou shall goeth and turneth watereth into wineth for thy own saketh".

What I'm saying is, if you are thinking that you can't read the bible because you don't understand it is an old excuse. There are many different versions written in plain English such as NIV (New International Version), NLV (New Living Version), ESV (English Standard Version), NKJV (New King James Version- there's still a few thy's and –eth's in this one) and even MSG (The Message) which is really a paraphrase telling you what the point of it all is.

If you like reading, the bible is just one huge story book telling of all the things God has done. It goes all the way back to when He first created Earth to when Jesus will come back. If you want to get to know God, think of the bible as His social media profile.

Talk to Him every day/as often as you can

What do you when you fall in love with someone? Call them ALL day! Every day! You call just to say hello or to say a commercial reminded you of them. You buy them special trinkets and devote all of your time and attention to making sure they know that they are loved. That's what God wants from you!

How would you feel if you went around giving people whatever is best for them and the only time they call is when they need something? Hmmp, living in Guilt and Shame you probably experienced that on a small level. How much bigger is the level on which God deals with this?

This lovey dovey, you-hang-up-no-you-hang-up-no-you-hang-up kind of affair is what God wants. That's what you have to do with God. You can't call him up or send Him an e-card, but you can spend time with Him prayer.

I like to do my praying early in the morning, a mid- day and a before bed prayer. These are like little fill ups throughout my day. Sometimes, you don't even have to say anything but just invite Him into your presence and spend some quiet time with Him. You can also spend time with God by reading His Word.

When you get a hot new fling or maybe when you first fell in love with your spouse, you wanted to be with them all the time and this relationship with God has to be more important than that. Unlike relationships, this one won't get old. You can tell God exactly how you feel, even if you are mad with Him and He will never hold it against you.

The more time you spend with God, the stronger you get and as you gain strength it becomes easier to not just talk back to Guilt and Shame, but to see their tricks from a mile away and avoid them.

Enlist support

I didn't mention getting a counselor or prayer partner for no reason. It will be vital to your success to have someone who can pray with and for you. Sometimes when we are trying to get our homes together, it's all we can do to get out of bed.

On those days, there will need to be someone you can call to encourage you. On those days you are second guessing yourself, there will need to be someone to equip you with tools and resources to clear your thinking.

I know a lot of people believe that if you have faith there won't be depression, anxiety or even guilt and shame. I agree to an extent but I also believe that mental health is a real thing that needs our attention as much as physical health.

Our prayer partners will talk to God and stand in the gap for us and (if need be) a counselor or therapist can equip us in other ways.

If you are believing in God for something but not doing all you can on your level, you might as well not believe. God is not a wish granter. If you say that you want to change how you think and who lives in your house, then in order for God to move, you have to move first. I believe (if you need it), that getting mental health assistance is a step in the right direction.

Use your affirmations, set ground rules

Your affirmations should be the rules of your everyday life. Just as a teacher hangs up classroom rules as a reminder, your affirmations should hang the same way so that even if Guilt and Shame come by for a visit, they see that it's a whole nother level to this thing.

If you choose "Seek the Lord with all your heart and lean not on your own understanding" as an affirmation, don't just go through life purposely trying not to understand things but SEEK THE LORD. That is a rule in your house! Read His word, spend time with Him, and join a bible based church.

If you choose "I do not have a spirit of fear but of power, love and self-control" don't go around pounding your chest trying to exert your little power over people. Power in this sense doesn't mean making people do what you want but resisting the enemy in his ploys against you. Having a spirit of power, love and self-control becomes a rule of your house.

Do Daily Housekeeping

In this eviction process, we acknowledged that Guilt and Shame were there and in order to do that we had to look around. We have to pull some dressers out, we had to get Saturday morning if you will. In order to avoid the Saturday morning process, we want to do this every day. Remember, the doorway to guilt and shame is unconfessed sin. Every day, at whatever time works best for you, think about something that could be festering within you. If it's not guilt or shame, is it one of their sub-tenants? Do a replay of your day and ask God for forgiveness and help in those areas.

I know this may seem like a lot, but the fact is that you have to want God more than anything in this world. Only God can truly satisfy your thirst for a better life. What you are searching for is Him and you have to make time for Him.

Keep track of your progress

My poems and journal entries are not in this book to show you that I can make words rhyme or that I have had bad days. They are to show you that having keepsakes to look back on makes it easy to see how far you've come. These entries serve as my before and after weight loss pictures so to speak. They also serve as a reminder of all of the things God has done for me. As I'm sitting here writing a book about the goodness of God, it's easy for me to remember those things.

If the book doesn't sell, it may be hard for me to deal with, I may begin to question God and if you go through hard times, chances are you will do the same. Having a journal of prayers sent and answered, of your emotional state and the joys you experience will serve as a reminder that God can do all things.

Having those writings will let you know that even in the hard times it's best to lean not on your own understanding. Having those writings will give you something to be thankful for because if this book doesn't sell a single copy, my deliverance proved by journal entries is enough to be thankful for in itself.

Celebrate small victories

There's an old saying that goes "Don't sweat the small stuff." In the case of this eviction, I want you to. Not the bad stuff, but the good stuff. Yes, celebrate. If you avoid a situation that you know will cause you guilt, celebrate. If you don't avoid that situation but you immediately confess your sin and accept your forgiveness, celebrate. If you have the courage to (in love and self-control) stand up for yourself, if only in a small way, celebrate.

Thinking that there will be one big turnaround moment is a set up. This will be an everyday mission and every day you should be able to find something to celebrate and encourage yourself about.

Do background checks on potential tenants

So while you are celebrating your small victories, don't let new tenants slip in unnoticed. While you have handled that anger issue and thinking about the people who hurt you doesn't make your blood boil anymore, if you feel like "If only they hadn't...." that could be the beginning for resentment and bitterness. Resentment/bitterness is the lingering feeling of being done wrong.

Resentment/bitterness is to anger what the dirty ring is around a bathtub after a bath. Though the water (anger) may not be there anymore, the here may be some residue remaining (resentment/bitterness).

Read what God says about that. If you read that someone else read this book and they had a tangible miracle and you think "Why didn't that happen for me?" that's sounds like the perfect setup for jealousy. Read what God has to say about that.

During your daily housekeeping, pay attention to all of these feelings. Don't go through this journey to get guilt and shame out and end up resentful and jealous! Who wins then?

Again, that's another rhetorical question. During your time getting to know God, see what he says about all of these possible sub-tenants. In the index of most bibles can lead you to specific scriptures on any negative feelings you may be having.

Invite new tenants

Finally, in your new, clean house, with your rules hanging up and windows open, you might just feel like having a party. Go ahead! Invite some tenants in to check out your space. If it's all clean and organized, they might just want to make camp there. Remember the tenants God wants us to have are the fruit of the spirit: peace, love, joy, patience, kindness, goodness, faithfulness, gentleness and self-control. How do you invite them over? Simple. The same way you evicted Guilt and Shame, ask God.

POST-EVICTION PRAYER

Dear God,

I give you me. I need your help. I need your strength. Please, if you don't help me I don't have anything else or a plan B. I'm all in, everything that you have allowed or not allowed I accept as a gift and thank you for it. I know that you are always at work, always in control and always making me a winner. Lord, I am on a mission for you. I'm not sure what it is but I'm down. I want to be included. Show me through scriptures, promptings from The Holy Spirit and people, what your will is for me.

Lord, I choose to be released from bitterness, anger, rage, unforgiveness, guilt and shame. I choose to walk in your footsteps to Heaven. I choose not be mad. I choose to forgive. I don't expect anything from anybody for we all fall short of the glory of God. All I expect is for you to take complete care of me because that's what your word says you will do. Lord, I ask you to bless all the offenders against me and those I have offended myself. Help me to keep my house in white box condition. Lord, I invite new thoughts from you into my house. Thank you for protection, forgiveness, deliverance and eviction.

Amen.

38676335R00083

Made in the USA
Columbia, SC
07 December 2018